Do The DAKI

A SEL PROGRAM FOR K-3 EDUCATORS

KELLY LESLIE & JOYCE TAM

FOREWORD BY DR. JACIE MASLYK

ISBN 978-1-7778205-1-0

To all the incredible educators who value a positive climate both in your classrooms and schools. We hope this resource is a support for the amazing work you do on a daily basis.

To all the students who we hope will enjoy and benefit from this program.

Acknowledgements

Unity is strength... when there is teamwork and collaboration, wonderful things can be achieved.

—Mattie Stepanek, age 13

We have always valued the importance of a team approach whether as an administrator leading a school or a classroom teacher in a classroom. This book would not be possible without the team of people who supported our ideas and vision to support the social emotional well-being of students.

Thank you Jacie Maslyk for your valued expertise and support, it was a pleasure working with you.

Thank you Wendy Dowling for being our supportive mentor. You have had a huge impact on our collaborative efforts.

Thank you Gail McDonald for your professional review and seeing the value of this resource from a principal's point of view.

Thank you Brenda Spencer, not only for your incredible support of the *Hannah and Bruno Series*, but for your kind review of *Do The DAKI*, as well.

Thank you Sue Oolup for being our cheerleader and editor! Your friendship, encouragement and support has meant the world to us.

Thank you Catherine MacCormack for your creative contributions.

Thank you Asher Kortes for your incredible coding skills and assistance creating the Escape Rooms. We know students will love them!

Contents

Foreword by Dr. Jacie Maslyk

If there has ever been a time to focus on the social emotional development of our young people, it is now. Our students have spent the last two school years in and out of school, learning through online, hybrid, and traditional models of instruction. They have persevered through challenges and are now ready to re-enter our classrooms. As a former school principal and central office administrator, I know that teachers are looking for ways to incorporate the social emotional development of their students in meaningful ways. As a mom, I hope that all schools will focus with intention on ensuring that ALL students feel safe and supported, this year and every year.

We will welcome students back with open arms and open hearts, embracing the opportunity to learn together again. It is our goal to establish and maintain a positive classroom climate where our students are ready to learn and grow. Unfortunately, some of our students may be returning to school with uncertainties, fears, and misconceptions. They may be hesitant about coming back to school, in general. We can equip them with the skills and strategies to head resiliently into this new school year--and this book can help make it happen!

With their combined school leadership and classroom experience, authors Kelly Leslie and Joyce Tam share a resource that will support learning in any K-3 classroom. They offer a practical approach to an important topic. Connecting children's literature, social emotional learning, and STEM strategies (all things that I am passionate about) the authors offer a framework for educators who also value the well-being and personal development of young people.

Their message is simple. Yes, there are differences in people, but let's focus on the positive differences. You will encounter people that are different from you, but let's greet them with acceptance. There may be people who aren't always nice, but you can approach everyone with kindness and understanding. When we see people on the fringe, we can reach out and ensure that they are included. The importance of positive differences, acceptance, kindness, and inclusion need to be present in our homes and communities, but especially in our schools.

Aligned with Kelly's children's book series, the DAKI program provides a way for teachers to incorporate lesson extensions to the books that teachers and students know and love. Stories like *Hannah's Hugs* and *Believe in Bruno* provide a context for discussing individuals with neurodiversity, physical challenges, and communication needs. These books share simple messages within heartfelt stories, making them the perfect fit for any primary classroom. Not only do the authors provide the context for this learning through these engaging stories, but they also offer lots of practical components for classroom use. From ready-to-use templates to lesson ideas, the book is a comprehensive and quality resource.

As an advocate for STEAM education, one of my favorite parts of the book are the connections to science, technology, engineering, art, and math. Incorporating creativity and design into social emotional learning helps students to make concrete connections as they use their imaginations to brainstorm, problem solve, and build. Students will activate critical thinking and communication skills as they collaborate to solve challenges and offer creative solutions. Whether constructing mazes or towers or using digital escape rooms, students will learn teamwork and leadership skills throughout the year. They will begin to develop a growth mindset and the understanding that they can tackle any problem that comes their way. SEL and STEM intersect in a way that we can support development in both areas as we build student engagement.

This is the time to build a sense of empathy and understanding in our students. This book presents the opportunity to foster resilience within our students, developing their motivation to learn and their ability to connect with others. This is a chance to deepen our students' sense of self and validate that there is a place for everyone within our classrooms. Through our open dialogue with students and activities that prompt learners to think, wonder, and do, we can develop skills in SEL and the content areas.

As you navigate through a variety of challenges this year, this book will provide the guidance needed for K-3 teachers to build relationships with their students, as well as reinforce positive connections among students. Offering focused instruction on positive differences, acceptance, kindness, and inclusion, this resource will equip you with the ideas, vocabulary, and hands-on activities to provide meaningful SEL instruction to students. Get ready to jump in and "Do the DAKI!"

Dr. Jacie Maslyk has been a teacher, reading specialist, elementary principal, and assistant superintendent. She is the author of educational resources such as Unlock Creativity, Steam Makers and most recently, Remaking Literacy. She is currently an Educational Consultant working with teachers, schools and school boards.

jaciemaslyk@gmail.com

Introduction

Thank you for embarking on a learning journey that, we hope, will transform your classrooms into a positive learning environment.

Our creation of the DAKI Program has been evolving for many years. If you will indulge us, we will provide a brief history to provide some context.

Kelly's Story.....

What I learned as a young teacher, in the early 90's, is where this personal journey began for me. I can recall, all too clearly, the class I had that provided an "AHA" moment for me. We were a grade 5/6 class of 32+ students...in a portable! To say times were interesting would be an understatement.

I approached my colleagues asking for help. One of them introduced me to the *Sharing Circle,* as it was termed back then. The activity has transformed throughout the years and evolved into something like *Tribes* of today. Basically, we would partake in a sharing circle every single morning to begin our day (fitting 32+ students in a circle on the floor of a portable was an interesting feat). It was here that we learned to actively listen to one another, share our opinions about an array of topics in a judgement-free environment. The most amazing transformation began to take hold in our classroom. Mutual respect, supporting one another and a collaborative, collegial environment was the result. The students were soon leading the circle, adhering closely to our established norms and were quite upset if we ever missed our morning ritual.

Fast forward to the final five years of my career. I was the Principal of a school that was undertaking an amalgamation. It was of the utmost importance to create a school-wide vision of unity, acceptance, inclusion, and teamwork as two schools became one. I learned so much from the incredible staff and students at that school. I was consistently in awe and inspired by the collective vision of the staff as we created a positive school climate.

My personal journey continued into my retirement. I have always been passionate about our students with special needs and breaking down barriers. Past experiences throughout my career, coupled with my desire to teach children about differences, acceptance, kindness, and inclusion at an early age took root. The result being the creation of the *Hannah Series* and the *Bruno Series*, picture books for children aged 4-8. The intent of each book is to support neurodiverse students in seeing themselves represented in print. Conversely, to teach neurotypical students about positive differences, acceptance, kindness, and inclusion.

Joyce's story.....

Throughout my 20+ years in teaching, it has always been important to me to teach about kindness and inclusion in my classroom. To show students that although people come from different walks of life, with different abilities and experiences in their backpacks, different struggles and strengths, that everyone has something valuable to contribute.

My amazing teaching partner, Sue, and I are always in search of learning opportunities for our students to show kindness and to build empathy. When Kelly started writing her picture books with a goal of increasing representation and highlighting the strengths of the neurodiverse community, we knew we had to incorporate them into our program. Her books easily tie to curriculum areas like coding, language arts, science, math and STEM. But more importantly, when we started to see the students connect to the characters, the books turned into a springboard for meaningful conversations about identity and the value of inclusion.

Soon, we found ourselves using the books to discuss the Zones of Regulation, making connections to personal fears and learning about different neurodiversities, like autism, with greater understanding. As Kelly published each new book, our students were always engaged. So when Kelly asked me to partner up to write this SEL program for her books, it was an easy YES.

Logistics of the Book

It is our combined stories and expertise that resulted in the creation of the DAKI Program. We hoped to create a simple, easy to follow program addressing the Ontario Ministry identified Social Emotional Learning (SEL) Skills. Joyce's experiences of using the picture books in her classroom has shown us that the students readily identify with the characters, especially Hannah. We incorporated these characters throughout the program, as a result. The goal is to provide a year-long program for educators that will impact self-esteem while accepting others through kindness and inclusion (i.e., impacting cohesion and collaboration).

Different lesson formats have been utilized throughout the book. Therefore, Chapters One and Two consist of single lessons numbered accordingly (at times, differentiated into K-1 and Gr. 2-3). Some lessons in Chapters Three and Four consist of the three part lesson plan (Minds On, Action, and Consolidation), as a few are more extensive. We hope you find both useful.

Note: The following graphics are used when lesson are differentiated according to grade levels.

SEL (Social Emotional Learning Skills) Curriculum Expectations

The program has been designed to address the areas of the Ontario SEL curriculum below. We have included differentiation through inquiry based activities and cross-curricular areas of focus where possible.

- identify and manage emotions
- express their feelings and understand the feelings of others
- identify and cope with stress and challenges
- develop personal resilience
- maintain positive motivation and perseverance
- build a sense of hope and the will to keep trying for their goals
- build relationships and communicate effectively
- support healthy relationships and respect diversity
- deepen their sense of self
- develop a sense of identity and belonging
- thinking critically and creatively
- support decision-making and problem solving (both individually and collectively)

CHAPTER ONE

DIFFERENCES

Using the Achievement Chart

We have included the Ontario Achievement Chart to align with the requirements of the Ontario Curriculum. Each *pillar* (i.e. Differences, Acceptance, Kindness, and Inclusion) will be represented via an example of a section on the Achievement Chart.

We will provide the areas of the Achievement chart in each chapter, highlighting the area of focus per lesson(s).

STRENGTH LIES IN DIFFERENCES, NOT IN SIMILARITIES.

—STEPHEN COVEY

The first set of lessons address Knowledge and Understanding. Through exercises addressing comparisons, students will begin to identify differences. More importantly, highlight positive differences in each comparison.

KNOWLEDGE AND UNDERSTANDING -identifying differences and how they can be seen in a positive light	THINKING
COMMUNICATION	APPLICATION

LESSON 1

The first step is for students to identify what differences are. As in the example that follows, teacher questioning helps students elicit one or two similarities, via a dual image comparison. The next, more crucial step, is to elicit what the **positive differences** are between the pictures.

The knowledge and understanding of the content is addressed when teacher questioning results in an alignment of the words POSITIVE with DIFFERENCES.

The chosen pictures are just an example. The purpose is to use pictures that are meaningful to your students. Ones they will identify with. (APPENDICES A1-A5)

POSITIVE DIFFERENCES

(APPENDICES A1-A5)

1. What are these? Tell me one thing about each one.

2. What positive things do you see about the sundae and the triple scoops on a waffle cone that make them the same?

3. What positive things do you see about the sundae and the triple scoops on a waffle cone that make them **different**?

4. Explain how each of their **positive differences** makes them special.

** All questions focus on **positive differences** only throughout the entire program.

The next set of lessons serve two purposes. One is to identify and compare positive traits of various characters. The second is to incorporate critical thinking through a challenge involving six characters from the books.

KNOWLEDGE AND UNDERSTANDING	THINKING
-identifying differences and how they can be seen in a positive light	-explore differences attaching purpose to each positive difference identified -use critical thinking and processing to match a character to a task. Justify chosen character with evidence from text.
COMMUNICATION	APPLICATION

LESSON 2

In this lesson, the goal is to recognize the similarities between Tempest and Zack from *Hannah's Little Sis*. But even more importantly, to identify their individual **positive differences**.

Tempest, is determined, outspoken, motivated, empathetic (didn't want to try out for soccer unless Zack could), perseverant and persistent (couldn't wait to talk to her sister Hannah when she was upset about Zack).

Zack, has strong spatial awareness (able to see where all the players are from the sidelines, and identify their strengths), is artistic, humourous, intelligent, a self advocate, possesses positive self-esteem, and demonstrates leadership skills as the coach.

Positive Differences

Sort the pictures into the columns according to Tempest and Zack's positive differences, otherwise known as their strengths. (APPENDICES A6, A7)

EXAMPLE

Positive Differences

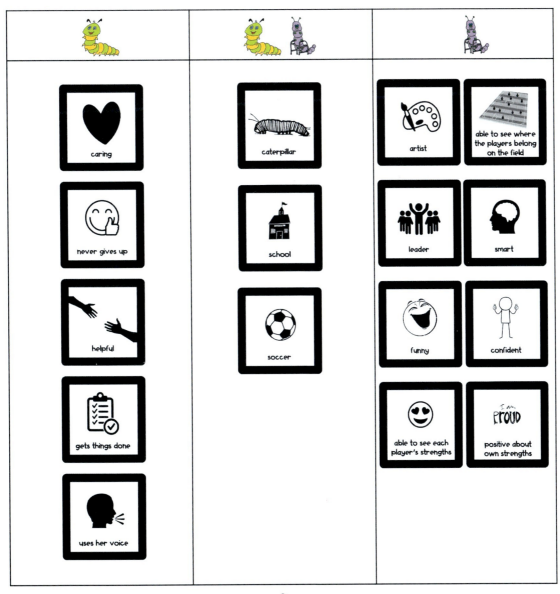

caring	caterpillar	artist	able to see where the players belong on the field
never gives up	school	leader	smart
helpful	soccer	funny	confident
gets things done		able to see each player's strengths	positive about own strengths
uses her voice			

LESSON 2A

In this Venn Diagram, the goal is to recognize the similarities between Hannah, as a butterfly, in *Hannah's Little Sis* and Kevin from *Kevin's Struggle*. More importantly, once again, is to identify their individual **positive differences**.

Hannah, is kind, caring, empathetic, helpful, accepting, inventive, persistent, cooperative, collaborative, and a good listener (this terminology has been transferred into child-friendly language in the Venn diagram, i.e. possible responses you would elicit from your students).

Kevin, has strong spatial awareness, is a problem solver, athletic, determined, a leader, and reflective.

Refer to the Venn Diagram on the next page.

Positive Differences

HANNAH'S LITTLE SIS
KEVIN'S STRUGGLE

(APPENDIX A8)

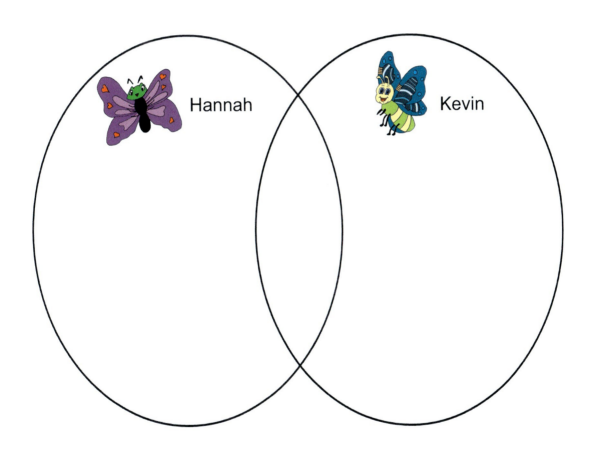

EXAMPLE

Positive Differences

HANNAH'S LITTLE SIS
KEVIN'S STRUGGLE

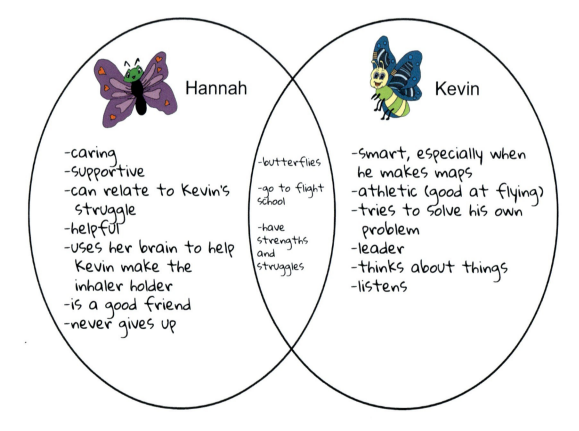

Hannah

-caring
-supportive
-can relate to Kevin's
 struggle
-helpful
-uses her brain to help
 Kevin make the
 inhaler holder
-is a good friend
-never gives up

-butterflies

-go to flight
 school

-have
 strengths
 and
 struggles

Kevin

-smart, especially when
 he makes maps
-athletic (good at flying)
-tries to solve his own
 problem
-leader
-thinks about things
-listens

LESSON 2B

In this Venn Diagram, the goal is to recognize the similarities between Kim and Bruno from *Believe in Bruno*. As always, please highlight the importance of their individual **positive differences.**

Kim is kind, caring, brave, helpful, accepting, determined, and perseveres (this terminology has been transferred into child-friendly language in the Venn diagram, i.e. possible responses you would elicit from your students).

Bruno is kind, a learner, likes superheros, strives for inclusion, wants to make friends (once again, these descriptors have been translated to possible child-friendly language).

Refer to the Venn Diagram on the next page.

Positive Differences

BELIEVE IN BRUNO

(APPENDIX A9)

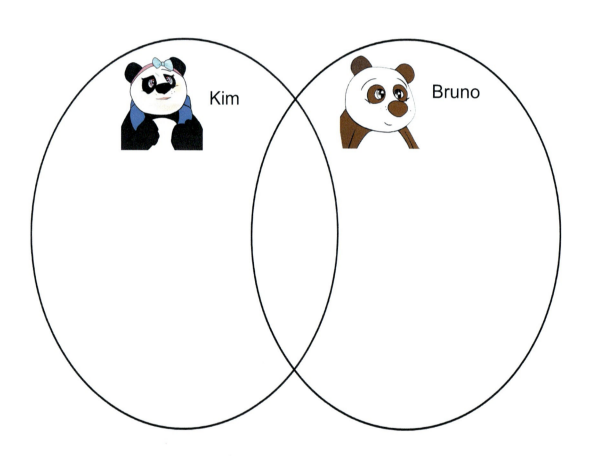

Kim

Bruno

EXAMPLE

Positive Differences

BELIEVE IN BRUNO

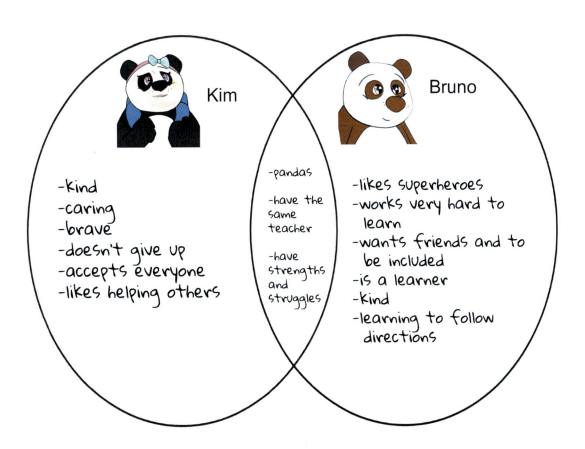

Kim
- kind
- caring
- brave
- doesn't give up
- accepts everyone
- likes helping others

- pandas
- have the same teacher
- have strengths and struggles

Bruno
- likes superheroes
- works very hard to learn
- wants friends and to be included
- is a learner
- kind
- learning to follow directions

LESSON 2C

In this Venn Diagram, the goal is to recognize the similarities between Tempest and Zack from *Hannah's Little Sis*, and Rylie from *Rylie the Riddler*. But even more importantly, to identify their individual **positive differences**.

Tempest, is determined, outspoken, motivated, empathetic (didn't want to try out for soccer unless Zack could), perseverant and persistent (couldn't wait to talk to her sister Hannah when she was upset about Zack).

Zack, has strong spatial awareness (able to see where all the players are from the sidelines, and identify their strengths), is artistic, humourous, intelligent, a self advocate, possesses positive self-esteem, and demonstrates leadership skills as the coach.

Rylie, is energetic (always running off to different places), funny (constantly telling jokes), a fast thinker in times of crises (developing a plan on his feet to rescue the primary caterpillars), cares about others (reassures the primary caterpillars not to worry), a problem solver and leader (takes a leadership role in carrying out his plan to rescue the primary caterpillars).

Refer to the Venn Diagram on the next page.

Positive Differences

*HANNAH'S LITTLE SIS
RYLIE THE RIDDLER*

(APPENDIX A10; BLANK TEMPLATES A11, A12)

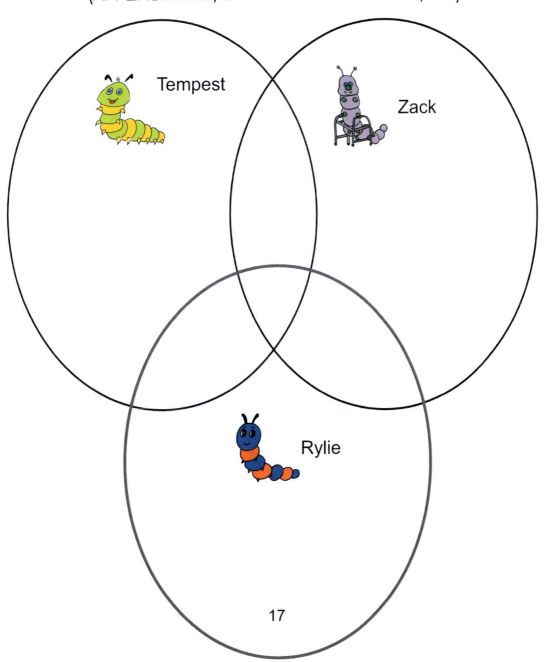

Tempest

Zack

Rylie

17

Positive Differences

HANNAH'S LITTLE SIS
RYLIE THE RIDDLER

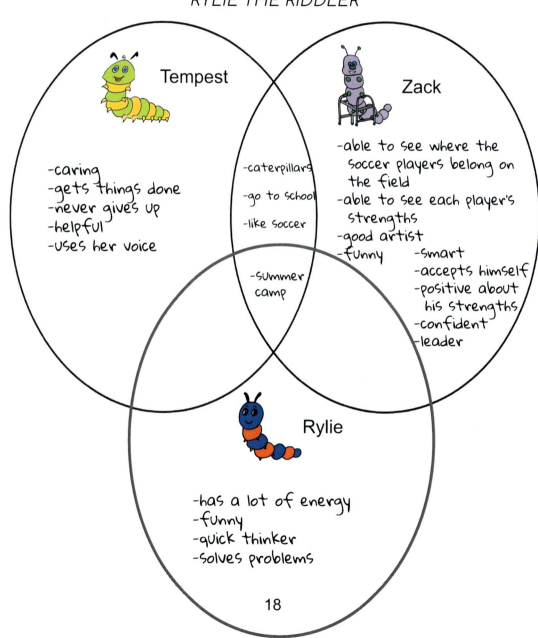

Tempest

-caring
-gets things done
-never gives up
-helpful
-uses her voice

-caterpillars
-go to school
-like soccer

-summer camp

Zack

-able to see where the soccer players belong on the field
-able to see each player's strengths
-good artist
-funny
-smart
-accepts himself
-positive about his strengths
-confident
-leader

Rylie

-has a lot of energy
-funny
-quick thinker
-solves problems

18

LESSON 3

The next set of challenges continues to address the Thinking construct of the Achievement Chart. The activities have been designed to support critical thinking challenges as well as to engage students in justifying their thinking related to **positive differences**.

The first challenge involves all seven characters studied to date (Tempest, Zack, Hannah, Kevin, Bruno, Kim, and Rylie). The group of friends are entering a corn maze building contest taking place in the country. The task is explained via different scenarios. The students select which character they think best suits each scenario given. Additionally, students should justify their thinking as to why they matched a particular character to a certain scenario based on their previously identified **positive differences**.

The next step is to put students into groups to build their own corn maze. Just as the characters in the previous activity, have each team decide what materials they will use (perhaps a good time for a class visit to the Makerspace). The students must ensure that each team member has a role. For example, one student might be Zack, who is artistic. That student could be the one who draws out the plans for the team. Just as the characters in the books, have your teams create their own maze for the other groups to navigate.

Each team can be timed taking turns going through each others' mazes. Every team must navigate the maze as one.

Using the scenarios provided below, discuss with students which character would be best suited to complete the task based on their **positive differences** (strengths).

WHO IS THE IDEAL CHARACTER FOR EACH JOB?
(possible answers are in the parentheses)

When Farmer Ken announces the contest, who will take the criteria and create the vision (i.e. the big picture) for the corn maze? (ZACK)

Once the plan for the maze has been approved, who will design the drawing for the maze? (KEVIN)

When the drawing is done, which two characters get started on the task right away, making paths in the cornfield quickly, according to the drawing? (TEMPEST OR RYLIE)

When the beating sun starts draining everyone's energy, who will encourage the team to keep going by giving helpful hugs? (HANNAH)

Who uses picture symbols when showing a friend how and where to cut the corn to make the paths? (KIM)

Once instructions are clear, who is amazing at working hard to create the maze? (BRUNO)

CHARACTERS:

Hannah   Zack   Tempest   Kevin

Rylie   Bruno   Kim

SETTING: Farm field in the country.

STEM CHALLENGE:

Using recycled materials or building materials available to you, as a team, design and create a corn maze.

Each character must use their **positive differences**, otherwise known as one of their **strengths**, to contribute to the team's success. Challenge students to increase level of difficulty to get through the maze.

LESSON 3A - EXTENSION (technology needed)

The same group of friends are stuck in an Escape Room. Again, select the character who is best suited to complete the task based on their **positive differences** previously identified.

To access the activity, copy and paste the following link in your browser for the Escape Room.   https://bit.ly/2XW5zar

To access the activity, copy and paste the following link in your browser for the Escape Room.   https://bit.ly/3gv5il6

The lessons pertaining to Communication in the Achievement Chart will have students working independently. They will identify and communicate their positive traits and align themselves with a character, based on common strengths.

KNOWLEDGE AND UNDERSTANDING	THINKING
-identifying differences and how they can be seen in a positive light	-explore differences attaching purpose to each positive difference identified -use critical thinking and processing to match a character to a task. Justify chosen character with evidence from text.
COMMUNICATION	APPLICATION
-identify self positive differences, align self with a character -communicate through pictures, words or both illustrating alignment of positive differences	

LESSON 4

We All Have Positive Differences...
What Are Mine?

Have students list three things they like to do and are good at. Put one strength (**positive difference**) in each bubble. (APPENDIX A13)

EXAMPLE

We All Have Positive Differences...
What Are Mine?

Have students list three things they like to do and are good at. Put one strength (**positive difference**) in each bubble.

Who Is Most Like Me?

Review the positive strengths of all the characters. Help students distinguish who is **most** like them based on similar positive traits. (APPENDIX A14)

Tempest	-caring -gets things done -never gives up -helpful -uses her voice
Zack	-able to see where the soccer players belong on the field -able to see each player's strength -good artist -funny -smart -accepts himself -positive about his strengths -confident -leader
Hannah	-caring -supportive -can relate to Kevin's struggle -helpful -uses her brain to help Kevin make the inhaler holder -is a good friend -never gives up

Who Is Most Like Me?

(APPENDIX A15)

Kevin	-smart, especially when he makes maps -athletic (good at flying) -tries to solve his own problem -leader -thinks about things -listens
Bruno	-likes superheroes -works very hard to learn -wants friends and to be included -is a learner -kind -learning to follow directions
Kim	-kind -caring -brave -doesn't give up -accepts everyone -likes helping others
Rylie	-lots of energy -funny -super fast thinker -can solve problems really well -really good at self-talk -likes helping others

My Twin (Character) and I

(APPENDIX A16)

My Strengths

Picture of
Self

My strengths are:

My Twin - Who is Most Like Me and Why

Picture of
Character

I am most like _____
because:

My Twin (Character) and I

EXAMPLE

My Strengths

My strengths are:

-funny
-smart
-like sports

My Twin - Who is Most Like Me and Why

I am most like <u>Zack</u> because:

-he is smart
-he likes sports, especially soccer
-he is nice and funny

Draw a picture of you and your twin on the left wings.
Identify your individual strengths on the right wings.
(APPENDIX A17)

EXAMPLE

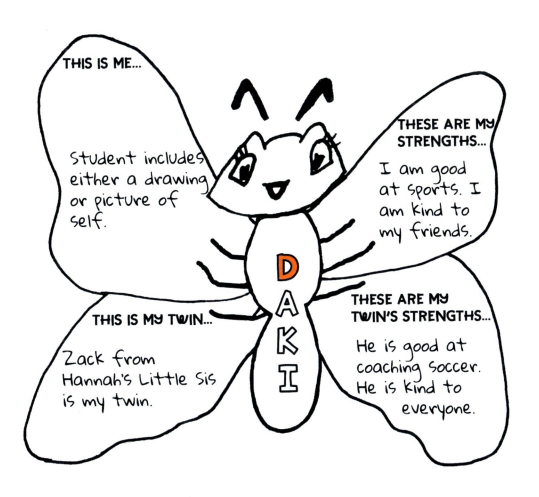

THIS IS ME...

Student includes either a drawing or picture of self.

THESE ARE MY STRENGTHS...

I am good at sports. I am kind to my friends.

D
A
K
I

THIS IS MY TWIN...

Zack from Hannah's Little Sis is my twin.

THESE ARE MY TWIN'S STRENGTHS...

He is good at coaching soccer. He is kind to everyone.

The lessons pertaining to Communication in the Achievement Chart will have students working in small groups. They will apply their positive differences in task completion.

KNOWLEDGE AND UNDERSTANDING	THINKING
-identifying differences and how they can be seen in a positive light	-explore differences attaching purpose to each positive difference identified -use critical thinking and processing to match a character to a task. Justify chosen character with evidence from text.
COMMUNICATION	APPLICATION
-identify self positive differences, align with a character -communicate through pictures, words or both illustrating alignment of positive differences	-students place themselves, or are placed, into groups of varying characters (i.e. various strengths) -each group completes an activity focusing on how their strengths helps the group in task completion

LESSON 5

COLLABORATIVE ACTIVITIES

It's time for the students to practice teamwork in their own groups. Either create new groups or have students work with the same team from the Corn Maze activity.

The next few pages will take you to some suggested activities that require students to collaborate.

The important point of the exercise is the follow-up discussion.

 Have students sit with their team members and tell how each person contributed their strengths to the activity.

 Ask team members to share how others' strengths in their group supported the team effort. Have each team fill out the template provided (Our Awesome Team).

Matching Positive Differences

This is a review before applying the same qualities to their group members. Match the character to the positive difference traits. More than one trait can be connected to a character. One has been done for you. (APPENDIX A18)

kind
supportive
smart
athletic
fast thinker
speaks up for others
funny
energetic
caring
includes others
leader
good listener
hard worker

34

Matching Positive Differences

Come up with your own words and match the character to the positive difference traits. More than one trait can be connected to a character. One has been done for you. (APPENDIX A19)

_____

_____

_____

_____

_____

_____

_____

_____

_____

_____

_____

hard worker

Collaborative Activities

The following are suggestions:

➤ Flip the Sheet

This is one activity that will get kids to bond and encourage creative thinking. Give the kids a flat tarp or bedsheet, and get them to stand over it. The challenge for them is to turn over the sheet until they are standing on the opposite side, without their feet touching the ground or stepping off the sheet. They'll have a blast strategizing on how to give the sheet an excellent ole flip! You can also divide the kids into two groups and have them race to see which group can do it first!

Reference: 23 Team Building Activities for Kids to Learn Teamwork (thequeenmomma.com)

➤ Sneak A Peek

Materials:
- Building blocks – you will need as many sets as the number of teams
- Space for kids to work

Number of participants: Six to eight teams of three kids each

Time required: 15 minutes

Instructions:
- Create a structure using building blocks, without the kids seeing it – you can do it in another room and bring it to the kids.
- Give each team one set of blocks. Show the structure you have created.
- One person from each team comes and takes a peek at the structure. They have ten seconds to look at it and memorize it.
- The team member will have to explain the structure to the others so that they can recreate it.
- If they don't get it right, another member from the team can go and take a peek at the structure and go back to helping the others.

Reference: 21 Fun Team Building Games And Activities For Kids (momjunction.com)

➤ Tallest Tower

Tallest tower challenges kids to build the tallest possible tower they can with whatever is available around them. This game can be played indoors.

How it helps:

This game encourages students to use their creativity to make their tower the tallest.

Materials:
- Books
- Tins
- Blocks

Anything else that is unbreakable can be used in building the tower.

Instructions:

- Children are in their previously identified groups.
- Give them the needed material for building their tower – they could also use other items in the room, with your permission, to complete their tower.
- On 'go', the teams start building a freestanding tower with the material.
- Give them ten minutes to complete the tower.
- Teams rotate to view each other's towers, making at least one positive comment about each.

Reference: 21 Fun Team Building Games And Activities For Kids (momjunction.com)

Our Awesome Team

Every person on a team is what makes it awesome!
Share one **positive difference** made by each person
on your team. For example, Ariya, you were helpful
with your organizational skills in getting everyone
started. Jeremiah, your ability to spatially visualize
helped the team.

As a team, match each member to one positive
difference. (APPENDIX A20)

Positive Differences   Team Member

_____   _____

_____   _____

_____   _____

_____   _____

_____   _____

_____   _____

CHAPTER TWO

ACCEPTANCE

The first set of lessons address Knowledge and Understanding. Through various exercises, students will begin to identify acceptance, both of self and others.

KNOWLEDGE AND UNDERSTANDING -students will identify the meaning of acceptance as it applies to self and others	THINKING
COMMUNICATION	APPLICATION

LESSON 1

MINDS-ON

This activity addresses the need for students to identify what **acceptance** means. A read aloud of *Don't Call Me Special*, by Pat Thomas (Hauppauge, 2002) could be used.

Through conversation and questioning the students can begin to explore their strengths and areas for growth. Dialogue and activities pertaining to growth mindset will focus on a paradigm shift of positive self-talk.

GROWTH MINDSET

What is a growth mindset? It's the first step in **self-acceptance**.

A growth mindset is a shift in perspective. It allows a child to shift from thinking they can't do something, to they can't do it, **yet**. A fixed mindset would see obstacles, whereas a growth mindset would see challenges as opportunities for growth. Mistakes become learning opportunities, getting them closer to **yet**.

Look at Tempest and Zack from *Hannah's Little Sis*. Zack is a perfect example of someone who accepts himself. When Tempest gets upset that Zack can't play soccer, he states, "I'm not sad, I've always been like this. It's normal for me. My legs may not move the same as yours, but my brain works just fine."

42

What are some things you're good at? What are some things you're still learning or working on? Include at least three things in each column. (APPENDIX B1)

Things I am good at...	Things I am still learning...

2-3

Choose two things you are still working on or still learning. What could you say to yourself to encourage yourself? (APPENDIX B2)

Things I am still learning...	Positive Self-Talk
I am still learning to	I can say
I am still learning to	I can say

Identify two things you are learning on the left wings, and what positive words you could say to yourself to keep trying, on the right wings. (APPENDIX B3)

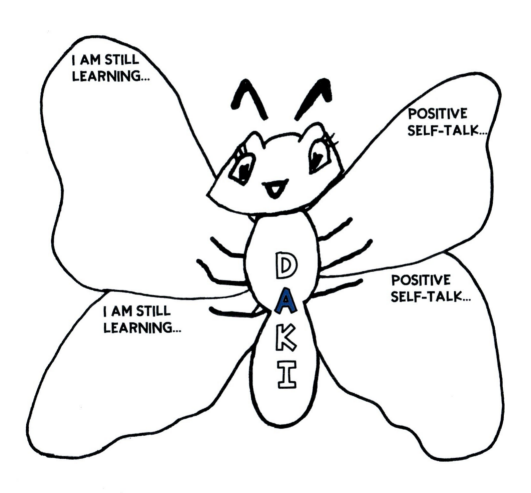

EXAMPLE

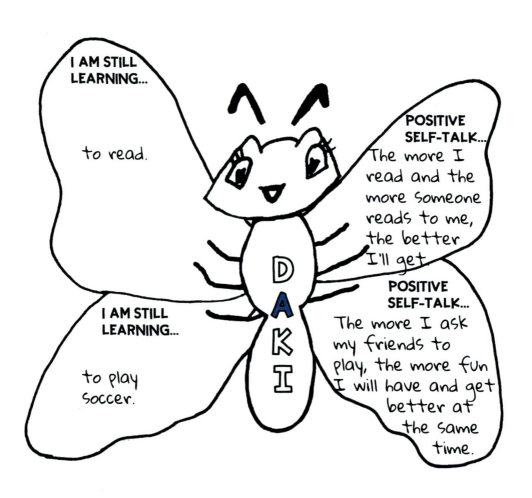

The second set of lessons address Thinking. Through various exercises, students will begin to identify behaviours exhibited by different characters that personify acceptance.

KNOWLEDGE AND UNDERSTANDING -students will identify the meaning of acceptance as it applies to self and others	THINKING -students will identify behaviours of self and others that contribute to acceptance
COMMUNICATION	APPLICATION

LESSON 2A
What are some things your friend does that makes you like him/her so much? (APPENDIX B4)

This is my friend.

EXAMPLE
What are some things your friend does that makes you like him/her so much?

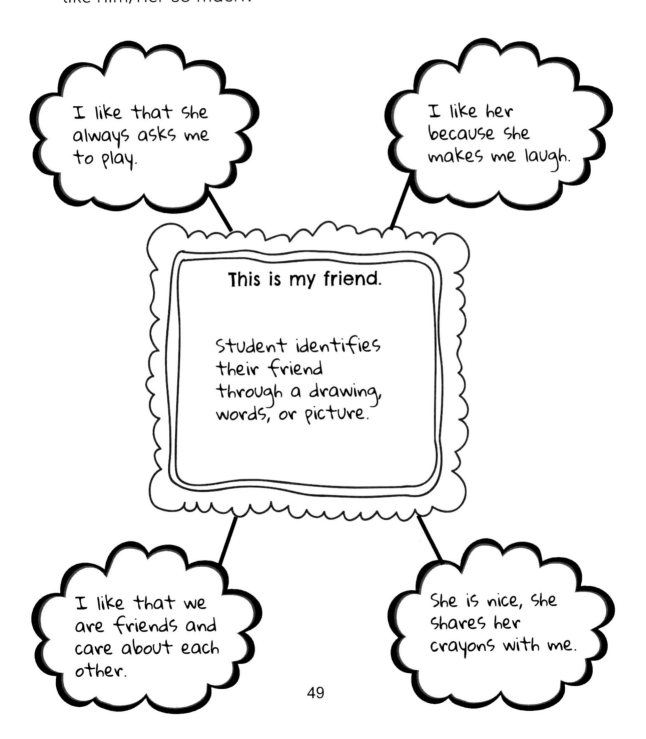

I like that she always asks me to play.

I like her because she makes me laugh.

This is my friend.

Student identifies their friend through a drawing, words, or picture.

I like that we are friends and care about each other.

She is nice, she shares her crayons with me.

49

LESSON 2B

Which characters from the books have some of the same behaviours as you, or your friend? Who are they and what do they do to show acceptance of others? (APPENDIX B5)

This is   .

EXAMPLE
Which characters from the books have some of the same behaviours as you, or your friend? Who are they and what do they do to show acceptance of others?

Feels good when she helps Bruno.

Wants to help Bruno by finding ways to connect with him.

This is Kim.

Is kind to Bruno by picking up his Superhero card for him.

Teaches others how to play with Bruno.

The third set of lessons address Communication. Students will identify acceptance-related vocabulary via different character points of view (POV). This can also be differentiated with the use of technology (i.e. iPad to record speech) or through the creation of skits.

KNOWLEDGE AND UNDERSTANDING	THINKING
-students will identify the meaning of **acceptance** as it applies to self and others	-students will identify behaviours of self and others that contribute to acceptance
COMMUNICATION	APPLICATION
-students will communicate different character's POVs pertaining to acceptance in a comic strip format	

LESSON 3

Present different scenarios to students through a POV (point of view) lens. For example, it's raining outside...what would the plants think of that? What would a child wearing rain boots think of that? What would a bride think of that on her wedding day?

The next exercise consists of comic strips. A picture from a scene in Rylie the Riddler is provided with speech bubbles. Once the scene is reviewed with the class, the teacher can then read the speech bubbles. The student's task is to draw the character (choosing from all six books) who is most likely to say what is in the bubble. Thus establishing a different point of view relative to each character.

Note: The explanation below the speech bubbles in the examples are possible teacher conversation starters.

In *Rylie The Riddler*, Rylie led the team in rescuing the primary caterpillars. Think about all the characters we know from the books. Who do you think would say the following? Draw a picture of each of them.

(APPENDIX B6)

> Rylie, you're such a super-fast thinker. It's like your brain moves as fast as a soccer ball down the field.

> I'm so proud of Rylie, I would love to give him a big hug.

EXAMPLE

In *Rylie The Riddler*, Rylie led the team in rescuing the primary caterpillars. Think about all the characters we know from the books. Who do you think would say the following? Draw a picture of each of them.

Rylie, you're such a super-fast thinker. It's like your brain moves as fast as a soccer ball down the field.

Tempest is a girl of action and appreciates how quickly Rylie took over; she values his quick thinking.

I'm so proud of Rylie, I would love to give him a big hug.

Hannah's strength is giving Rylie a hug to show her appreciation of the wonderful thing he did.

In *Rylie The Riddler*, Rylie led the team in rescuing the primary caterpillars. Think about all the characters we know from the books. Who do you think would say the following? Draw a picture of each of them.

(APPENDIX B7, BLANK TEMPLATE B8)

I'm so amazed by how brave Rylie is, he wasn't scared at all. His self-talk must have really helped him.

I like Rylie, I want him for a friend.

EXAMPLE

In *Rylie The Riddler*, Rylie led the team in rescuing the primary caterpillars. Think about all the characters we know from the books. Who do you think would say the following? Draw a picture of each of them.

> I'm so amazed by how brave Rylie is, he wasn't scared at all. His self-talk must have really helped him.

Kim is proud of Rylie and recognizes the self-talk strategy that helped her when she was afraid.

> I like Rylie, I want him for a friend.

Bruno is recognizing friends and is able to tell Rylie he would like him as a friend because of the good things he sees in him.

LESSON 3

Scene: In *Rylie The Riddler*, Rylie led the team in rescuing the primary caterpillars.

The next exercise consists of comic strips. Review the scene from *Rylie the Riddler* with the class. The students can then complete the comic strips. They are to create the words that might be said to Rylie from the character's point of view, relative to their individual **strengths**.

In *Rylie The Riddler*, Rylie led the team in rescuing the primary caterpillars. Think about what each character would say to Rylie from their point of view, and based on their own individual strengths. Why would their words be different?

(APPENDIX B9- B11)

Kevin

Zack

EXAMPLE

In *Rylie The Riddler*, Rylie led the team in rescuing the primary caterpillars. Think about what each character would say to Rylie from their point of view, and based on their own individual strengths. Why would their words be different?

Kevin: Hey Rylie, way to get the butterflies together to lift the branch. Glad no one got hit by lightning.

Zack: Wow, Rylie. You got everyone moving so quickly on the ground, I thought I was at the Indy 500!

The fourth set of lessons address Application. Students will be presented with different speech and thought bubbles (the following are just examples - you might want to choose topics more pertinent to your class). K-1 students hold a "thumbs up" or "thumbs down" picture to illustrate if they agree or disagree with the teacher's prompts. Gr. 2-3 students identify the thought or speech bubble they disagree with most. They then defend their point of view with evidence from the text.

KNOWLEDGE AND UNDERSTANDING	THINKING
-students will identify the meaning of **acceptance** as it applies to self and others	-students will identify behaviours of self and others that contribute to **acceptance**
COMMUNICATION	APPLICATION
-students will communicate different character's POVs pertaining to **acceptance** in a comic strip format	-students will identify with statements they agree/disagree with and justify their answers

LESSON 4A

Below are some statements you can make to the students. Have them hold up the thumbs up to show he/she agrees or thumbs down to show he/she doesn't agree, after each statement. Follow-up conversations can garner their opinions as to why they agree or disagree (i.e. hearing their friends' point of views. These are just suggestions as you may decide on statements more pertinent to your class).
(APPENDIX B12)

Cats are better than dogs

I brought in a toy for show-and-tell and only I get to play with it.

If I have an idea, I should get to share it first.

If I don't like what someone is saying, I don't have to listen to them.

LESSON 4B
Select an opinion that you **disagree** with, the most. Find evidence from the text to prove your opposing opinion. Choose a way to show it. (APPENDIX B13)

These are some examples of possible teacher prompts for you. Select an opinion that you disagree with, the most. Find evidence from the text to prove your opposing opinion. Choose a way to show it.

LESSON 4C

Once again, these are possible teacher prompts. They are suggestions of how you might differentiate the culminating task through choice. Ways for students to diversify their defense of their opposing opinion that showcases **acceptance** with evidence from the text.

Have students complete an Exit Ticket to share what they have learned. (APPENDIX B14)

EXIT TICKET

You've just completed a creative piece to support an opinion you feel strongly about. As a result, what is the POSITIVE IMPACT this could have on you and on others?

I know that my opinion is important and can be shared in a respectful way.

EXIT TICKET

You've just completed a creative piece to support an opinion you feel strongly about. As a result, what is the POSITIVE IMPACT this could have on you and on others?

CHAPTER THREE

KINDNESS

BE KIND WHENEVER POSSIBLE. IT IS ALWAYS POSSIBLE.

—THE 14TH DALAI LAMA

The first set of lessons address Knowledge and Understanding. Through various exercises, students will learn to identify kind acts and the feelings/emotions associated with them.

KNOWLEDGE AND UNDERSTANDING -identify and clarify the meaning of kindness in various ways	THINKING
COMMUNICATION	APPLICATION

LESSON 1

MINDS ON

Generate a conversation with your class, or via a sharing circle, about the times they have either given and/or received, kindness. Elicit the feelings they experienced in both situations. Record key words of their responses and highlight commonalities of emotions.

ACTION

Students will fill in Hannah butterflies identifying one act of kindness they received and one they have given on the left wings. Each act will include a connection about the corresponding feelings/emotions they experienced as a result. Write or draw the impact on the right wings.

CONSOLIDATION

The focus of the consolidation phase is a cause and effect relationship. Acts of kindness from each of the books is reviewed. The students' task is to identify the scene and related emotions (K-1) or impact (Gr. 2-3).

Students are provided a problem from each book and a follow-up question addressing a corresponding act of kindness. They then colour the appropriate emotion the character felt before and after the act of kindness.

Extension: (Point of View): Tempest pulled Zack's chair, opened the door, got him paper. She was trying to show kindness towards him, to help him. Did Zack see it as that?

Students are provided a problem from each book. The students identify the impact of the act, applying their understanding of how our actions affect others.

LESSON 1 - ACTION

Identify an act of kindness you have received and one that you have have given on the left wings. What feelings or emotions did you experience as a result? Write or draw the impact on the right wings. (APPENDIX C1)

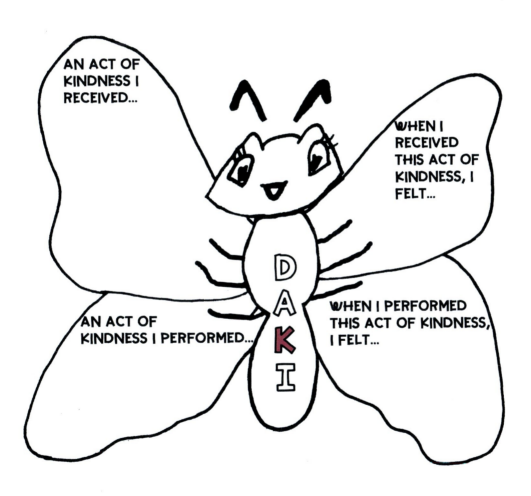

EXAMPLE

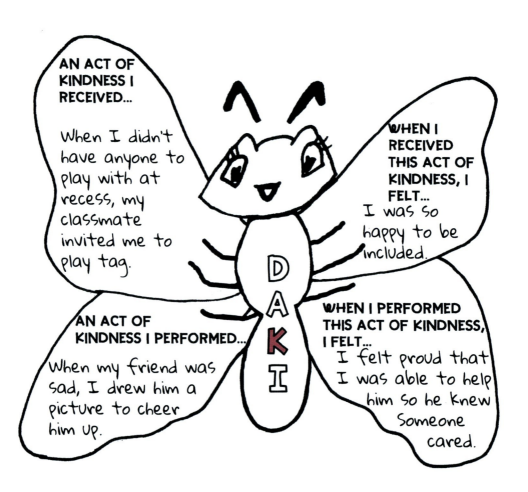

AN ACT OF KINDNESS I RECEIVED...

When I didn't have anyone to play with at recess, my classmate invited me to play tag.

WHEN I RECEIVED THIS ACT OF KINDNESS, I FELT...
I was so happy to be included.

AN ACT OF KINDNESS I PERFORMED...

When my friend was sad, I drew him a picture to cheer him up.

WHEN I PERFORMED THIS ACT OF KINDNESS, I FELT...
I felt proud that I was able to help him so he knew someone cared.

D A K I

LESSON 1 - **CONSOLIDATION** (APPENDIX C2)

PROBLEMS	ACTS OF KINDNESS	ANSWERS
HANNAH'S HUGS Hannah is scared to go into her cocoon.	What act of kindness did Kyle perform?	
HANNAH'S LITTLE SIS The team needs coaching.	What act of kindness did Zack perform?	
KEVIN'S STRUGGLE Kevin couldn't carry his inhaler during the long migration.	What act of kindness did Hannah perform?	
RYLIE THE RIDDLER The primary caterpillars are stuck in their tent during the storm.	What act of kindness did Rylie perform?	
BELIEVE IN BRUNO Bruno becomes upset at school.	What act of kindness did Kim perform?	
READY, SET, STOP! Bruno isn't able to participate in the Triple B Games due to safety reasons.	What act of kindness do Kim and Damian perform?	

EXAMPLE - CONSOLIDATION

PROBLEMS	ACTS OF KINDNESS	ANSWERS
HANNAH'S HUGS Hannah is scared to go into her cocoon.	What act of kindness did Kyle perform?	Kyle hugged Hannah and made her feel better.
HANNAH'S LITTLE SIS The team needs coaching.	What act of kindness did Zack perform?	Zack used his skill to individually help each player.
KEVIN'S STRUGGLE Kevin couldn't carry his inhaler during the long migration.	What act of kindness did Hannah perform?	Hannah helped Kevin make a holder for his inhaler.
RYLIE THE RIDDLER The primary caterpillars are stuck in their tent during the storm.	What act of kindness did Rylie perform?	Rylie led the team to lift the log that was blocking the tent.
BELIEVE IN BRUNO Bruno becomes upset at school.	What act of kindness did Kim perform?	Kim befriend Bruno.
READY, SET, STOP! Bruno isn't able to participate in the Triple B Games due to safety reasons.	What act of kindness do Kim and Damian perform?	Kim and Damian come up with a way to get Bruno to stop running.

LESSON 1 - CONSOLIDATION

How do the characters feel before and after the act of kindness. Colour the emoji you feel best represents the feeling. (APPENDIX C3)

Problems	How does the character feel?	Act of Kindness	How does the character feel after?
HANNAH'S HUGS Hannah is scared to go into her cocoon.	sad / scared or worried	After Kyle hugs Hannah.	calm / happy
HANNAH'S LITTLE SIS The team needs coaching.	sad / scared or worried	After Zack becomes the soccer coach.	calm / happy
KEVIN'S STRUGGLE Kevin couldn't carry his inhaler during the long migration.	sad / scared or worried	After Hannah helps Kevin build a holder for his inhaler for the migration trip.	calm / happy

LESSON 1 - CONSOLIDATION (cont'd)

How do the characters feel before and after the act of kindness. Colour the emoji you feel best represents the feeling. (APPENDIX C4)

Problems	How does the character feel?	Act of Kindness	How does the character feel after?
RYLIE THE RIDDLER The primary caterpillars are stuck in their tent during the storm.	sad / scared or worried	After Rylie leads the rescue of the primary caterpillars.	calm / happy
BELIEVE IN BRUNO Bruno becomes upset at school.	sad / scared or worried	After Kim befriends Bruno.	calm / happy
READY, SET, STOP! Bruno isn't able to participate in the Triple B Games due to safety concerns.	sad / scared or worried	After Kim and Damian prepare Bruno for the Triple B Games..	calm / happy

LESSON 1 - CONSOLIDATION

The focus of the consolidation phase is a cause and effect relationship. Acts of kindness from each of the books is reviewed. The student's task is to identify its impact. (APPENDIX C5)

Book Title/Act of Kindness	Impact
HANNAH'S HUGS Hannah hugged her little sister when she fell and scraped her knees.	
HANNAH'S LITTLE SIS Tommy asked Zack to be a coach for the team.	
KEVIN'S STRUGGLE Kevin worked really hard and created a new map for his class.	
RYLIE THE RIDDLER Rylie saved the primary caterpillars.	
BELIEVE IN BRUNO Kim taught her classmates ways to play with Bruno.	
READY, SET, STOP! Bruno drew a picture for Kim.	

LESSON 1 - CONSOLIDATION

The focus of the consolidation phase is a cause and effect relationship. Acts of kindness from each of the books is reviewed. The student's task is to identify its impact.

Book Title/Act of Kindness	Impact
HANNAH'S HUGS Hannah hugged her little sister when she fell and scraped her knees.	Her sister felt better and stopped crying.
HANNAH'S LITTLE SIS Tommy asked Zack to be a coach for the team.	Zack's strengths were recognized and he was included.
KEVIN'S STRUGGLE Kevin worked really hard and created a new map for his class.	Everyone in the class was able to participate in the migration journey.
RYLIE THE RIDDLER Rylie saved the primary caterpillars.	The primary caterpillars were safe and no longer afraid.
BELIEVE IN BRUNO Kim taught her classmates ways to play with Bruno.	Bruno was included.
READY, SET, STOP! Bruno drew a picture for Kim.	Kim was touched and her heart felt full from his gift.

The second set of lessons address Thinking. Through various exercises students will start to think critically and/or creatively through acts of kindness .

KNOWLEDGE AND UNDERSTANDING -identify and clarify the meaning of kindness in various ways	THINKING -students begin to use their knowledge about acts of kindness in creative ways through critical thinking
COMMUNICATION	APPLICATION

K-I

LESSON 2

The following are some ideas that encourage creativity:

KINDNESS ROCKS!

Paint rocks with pictures and positive messages. A nice gesture could be to place rocks in the community for others to find or give to a friend or family member.

KINDNESS BOOKMARKS.

Design a bookmark with kind words and pictures. Place them in library books for readers to find.

LESSON 2

COMPANY OF KINDNESS

This exercise can be conducted as a whole class. Its purpose is to access prior knowledge and continue to make connections in preparation for the culminating activity.

The first charts are to help students identify acts of kindness relative to their impact. (APPENDICES C6, C7). The final row is left blank to generate student ideas, focusing on acts of kindness that can make a larger impact.

This lesson will then lead to the culminating task, whereupon students are the VPs of their own Kindness Companies (APPENDIX 8).

In this lesson, students will use the acts of kindness from the books to decide whether these acts are easy or hard to perform. The purpose is to help them grasp the idea that they can easily perform little acts of kindness that can impact others. (APPENDIX C6)

Act of Kindness	How hard is it to do? easy or hard	What is the IMPACT? (write a sentence)	Number Impacted one or many	IMPACT big or little?
HANNAH'S LITTLE SIS Tempest opens the door for Zack.				
BELIEVE IN BRUNO Kim picks up Bruno's superhero card.				
HANNAH'S LITTLE SIS Zack coaches the team.				

Act of Kindness	How hard is it to do? easy or hard	What is the IMPACT? (write a sentence)	Number Impacted one or many	IMPACT big or little?
KEVIN'S STRUGGLE Hannah encourages Kevin to share about his asthma.				
KEVIN'S STRUGGLE Kevin makes a map for the migration journey.				
RYLIE THE RIDDLER: Rylie creates a team to lift the fallen branch.				
READY, SET, STOP! Bruno draws a picture for Kim.				
Come up with your own example:				

EXAMPLE

Some boxes have been filled in for you.

Act of Kindness	How hard is it to do? easy or hard	What is the IMPACT? (write a sentence)	Number Impacted one or many	IMPACT big or little?
HANNAH'S LITTLE SIS Tempest opens the door for Zack.	easy	Zack could easily get into the classroom.	one	little
BELIEVE IN BRUNO Kim picks up Bruno's superhero card.	easy	Bruno realized his friend can help him.	one	big
HANNAH'S LITTLE SIS Zack coaches the team.				

EXAMPLE
Some boxes have been filled in for you.

Act of Kindness	How hard is it to do? easy or hard	What is the IMPACT? (write a sentence)	Number Impacted one or many	IMPACT big or little?
KEVIN'S STRUGGLE Hannah encourages Kevin to share about his asthma.				
KEVIN'S STRUGGLE Kevin makes a map for the migration journey.	hard	Kevin impacted the whole class for the migration journey	many	big
RYLIE THE RIDDLER: Rylie creates a team to lift the fallen branch.	hard	The primary caterpillars were rescued.	many	big
READY, SET, STOP! Bruno draws a picture for Kim.				
Come up with your own example:				

CREATE A COMPANY OF KINDNESS

Arrange students in groups of four.

The following are the instructions per group.
You are the VPs of a Company of Kindness. As a team, you will:

1.   Give your company a name.
2.   Create an act of kindness that will impact part of your community.
3.   Write your business plan (once you decide on your company's act of kindness, how will you make it happen?).
4.   Create an advertisement through a poster, pamphlet, slide show, video, commercial etc.

The ad/presentation must include:

1.   Company Name
2.   Company Logo
3.   Summary of your plan/idea
4.   Who your plan impacts

COMPANY OF KINDNESS

Your business plan for your company's act of kindness. Remember it must impact someone, or a group, in your community. (APPENDIX C8)

VP Names	
Company Name	
Plan/Idea - Act of Kindness	
Who Will It Impact, and How?	
Company Logo (Design)	

The third set of lessons address Communication. Through various exercises, students will communicate for different audiences and purposes.

KNOWLEDGE AND UNDERSTANDING -identify and clarify the meaning of kindness in various ways	THINKING -students begin to use their knowledge about acts of kindness in creative ways through critical thinking
COMMUNICATION -students will communicate their knowledge of acts of kindness and impact through various modalities	APPLICATION

LESSON 3

Collectively as a class, create a Kindness Caterpillar. Every time someone in the class performs an act of kindness, the receiver can draw or write that act of kindness on a circle (body part) to add to the growing caterpillar. (APPENDIX C9)

My friend helped me when I was hurt.

My friend played with me at recess.

LESSON 3

The VPs of each company will pitch their idea to the Board of Directors (i.e., present their business plan to the class). Below is an example of a rubric for this assessment. (APPENDIX C10)

COMPANY OF KINDNESS RUBRIC

Categories	Level 4	Level 3	Level 2	Level 1
Knowledge and Understanding	Demonstrated a clear and cohesive understanding of their chosen act of kindness and the scale of its impact on a community	Demonstrated understanding of their chosen act of kindness and its impact on a community	Demonstrated understanding of their chosen act of kindness and its impact on a community, with support	Began to demonstrate understanding of their chosen act of kindness and its impact on a community, with support
Thinking	Planned a detailed Company of Kindness action plan and was cognizant of the critical thinking skills used (i.e., making inferences)	Planned and applied critical thinking skills to develop a Company of Kindness action plan	Planned and applied critical thinking skills to develop a Company of Kindness action plan, with support	Began to plan a Company of Kindness action plan, with support
Communication	Organized and expressed ideas in business plan and advertisement, with creativity and detail	Organized and expressed ideas in business plan and advertisement	Organized and expressed ideas in business plan and advertisement, with support	Began to organize and express ideas in business plan and advertisement, with support
Application	Made meaningful connections between Company of Kindness action plan and the impact it would have on their chosen community	Made connections between Company of Kindness action plan and the impact it would have on their chosen community	Made connections between Company of Kindness action plan and the impact it would have on their chosen community, with support	Began to make connections between Company of Kindness action plan and the impact it would have on their chosen community, with support

The fourth set of lessons address Application. Through various exercises the students will work as a class to connect acts of kindness to social justice issues (i.e., text-to-world).

KNOWLEDGE AND UNDERSTANDING	THINKING
-identify and clarify the meaning of kindness in various ways	-students begin to use their knowledge about acts of kindness in creative ways through critical thinking
COMMUNICATION	APPLICATION
-students will communicate their knowledge of acts of kindness and impact through various modalities	-students will make text-to-world connections through the application of acts of kindness

K-1

LESSON 4

MINDS ON

Show the video 10 Random Acts of Kindness for Kids by The Cohen Show as an example of acts of kindness performed by two young children.
(https://www.youtube.com/watch?v=OBbyjZdOsGo)

Brainstorm with students regarding what acts of kindness they could do individually, then as a group. Decide upon an act of kindness they would like to do as a class that would impact their school.

ACTION

Create a plan with your students. Fill out the template (example on the next page) with the class. Assign responsibilities to groups of students.

CONSOLIDATION

Execute the act of kindness and celebrate their success, i.e., the impact they made on others.

LESSON 4

OUR ACT OF KINDNESS
PLANNING SHEET

(APPENDIX C11)

Team Name:

Act of Kindness:	
Materials:	
Jobs:	
Group One (Names)	
Group Two (Names)	
Group Three (Names)	
Group Four (Names)	
Group Four (Names)	

OUR ACT OF KINDNESS
PLANNING SHEET

Team Name: The Cool Kindness Kids

Act of Kindness:	Make chalk games for the whole school on the primary and junior school yards.
Materials:	chalk
Jobs:	
Group One (Names)	Research 3 different games for primary kids.
Group Two (Names)	Research 3 different games for junior kids.
Group Three (Names)	Choose one game and colour of chalk and create the game.
Group Four (Names)	Choose a game and different colour of chalk and create the game.
Group Four (Names)	Choose a game and different colour of chalk and create the game.
Whole Class	Create posters/announcements to advertise your act of kindness to the entire school.

LESSON 4

MINDS ON

Discuss social justice issues and resulting acts of kindness. Some examples include: affordable housing (Habitat for Humanity), access to water in third world countries (Walk in Her Shoes), addressing poverty (Food Banks).

Note: This could also be a good opportunity to discuss the feasibility of the business plans they created.

ACTION

Support the students in reaching a class consensus around a specific social justice issue. Develop a plan that will impact others through kindness.

CONSOLIDATION

Execute the plan.

The following are snippets from a cross-curricular social justice initiative Joyce and Sue implemented in their Grade 2 classrooms. Please reference the UN's 17 Goals for Sustainable Development (https://sdgs.un.org/goals) to create your own global citizenship, global consciousness and social justice initiative pertinent to your grade level, curriculum, and class consensus.

Curriculum Expectations Covered:

- Social Studies (People and Environments: Global Communities)
- Science (Air and Water)
- Math (Financial Literacy: recognition of coins, sorting coins; Number: skip counting by 5s, 10s, 25, 100s, addition)
- Art (3D works of art with different mediums)
- Reading and Writing
- Critical Thinking, synthesizing information

This strand pairs nicely with the Ontario Grade 2 Science unit on Air and Water (the right to clean water), as well as connections to Language Arts, Math, and Visual Arts.

LESSON 4

What do you already know about the world? What do you wonder?

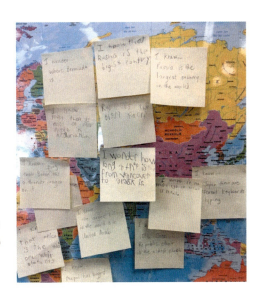

♦ **Figure 3.1** Students share their knowledge and wonders about the world. "I wonder how long a trip is from Vancouver to Alaska." "I know Russia is the largest country in the world."

WHAT DOES IT MEAN TO BE GLOBAL

After reading *What Does It Mean To Be Global* by Rana DiOrio (Little Pickle Press, 2009), the class co-created a list of what it means to be global. Selecting one item from the list, students created a plasticine representation in the style of Barbara Reid.

♦ **Figure 3.2** Being global means learning about traditions like Kwanzaa.

CARING PEOPLE AND IMPACT

After reading *I Can Make a Difference* by Miriam Laundry (Simon & Schuster, 2014), students thought about the impact they could make on other people, places, and the world.

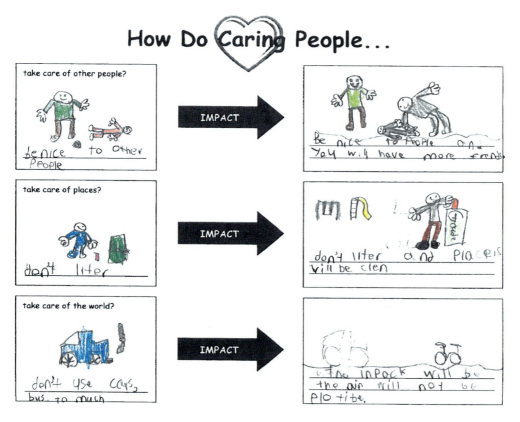

♦ **Figure 3.3** Student sample showing how caring people take care of each other, places, and the world.

APPRECIATING OUR DIFFERENCES

Looking at clothing, homes and food, students researched what different countries and cultures value with an emphasis on **positive differences**.

♦ **Figure 3.4** Clothing around the world.

Ee is for Edamame

Edamame means "stem bean" in Japanese. It is a soy bean that is green and fuzzy. There are 2 to 3 beans in a pod. Edamame grows from seeds in soil and sprouts from vines out of the ground. It grows in warm climates. Edamame is fast and easy to cook. To cook edamame you boil it for 5 minutes and sprinkle a little bit of salt on it. Edamame is also very healthy. It is very low in sodium and a very good source of vitamin K.

♦ **Figure 3.6** Foods around the world.

♦ **Figure 3.5** Homes around the world.

CANADA VS. AFRICA

After a unit on mapping, students took a closer look at Canada vs. Africa. At the same time, we were learning about the Air and Water in Science. Very quickly, they learned that not everyone has access to clean water (in our own province, and around the world). The second half of this unit focused on learning about the water conditions (lack of), conservation, sustainability and a call to action.

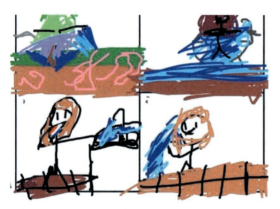

♦ **Figure 3.7** Foods around the world.

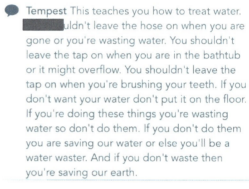

💬 **Tempest** This teaches you how to treat water. [redacted]uldn't leave the hose on when you are gone or you're wasting water. You shouldn't leave the tap on when you are in the bathtub or it might overflow. You shouldn't leave the tap on when you're brushing your teeth. If you don't want your water don't put it on the floor. If you're doing these things you're wasting water so don't do them. If you don't do them you are saving our water or else you'll be a water waster. And if you don't waste then you're saving our earth.

After reading *One Hen* by Katie Smith Milway (Kids Can Press, 2008), students thought critically about what they would rather have, to make the biggest impact about sustainability. They used the Critical Thinking strategy "Judge the Better or Best".

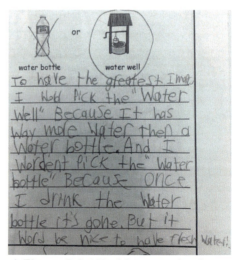

To have the greatest Impac, I Wold PiCK the "Water Well" BeCause It has Way mole Water then a Water bottle. And I Wordent PiCK the "Water bottle" BeCause once I drink the Water bottle it's gone. But it Word be nice to have fresh Water.

♦ **Figure 3.8** Would a water bottle or water well have the greatest impact?

TAKE ACTION

With a deeper understanding about the lack of access to water, or clean water, it was time to take action and help. We simulated a smaller version of Walk In Her Shoes. Collectively, students walked the necessary steps that a girl or woman in a developing country would need to take in order to collect water for her family.

Students shared their concerns with others to create awareness.

♦ **Figure 3.9**
Student letter to a staff member.

THE BIG EVENT

♦ **Figure 3.10** Students participating in Walk In Her Shoes.

Students used pedometers to track their steps. In pairs they walked 2500 steps each (the 5000 steps needed to get to water) with empty buckets, and then walked another 2500 steps each, carrying buckets of water half filled (the 5000 steps to get back home).

They had the opportunity to experience first hand what it's like to be a girl or woman in a developing country collecting water for their family.

MATH CONNECTIONS

Students totalled the loose change they raised. Once the money was added, students had to decide collectively how the money should be spent to create the biggest impact.

Enough money has been donated by the grade two students throughout the last five years to purchase 10 water wells for families.

♦ **Figure 3.11** Each table group provided data for their pile of coins.

We have raised _____ through Walk In Her Shoes for Care Canada. We know that:

$40.00 can buy drought-resistant seeds to help farmers produce food for their families when there is no rain.

$60.00 can buy provide clean water for a family to stay healthy.

$70.00 can send a girl to school for a year to earn an education.

$450 can buy a water pump that can provide clean, safe water to a whole community closer to home.

How might we donate this money to achieve the greatest IMPACT in a developing country? Would you want to support a community, school-aged children, families or a combination of these choices? **WHY?**

_____

_____

♦ **Figure 3.12** Students had to decide and justify which scenario would create the biggest impact.

CHAPTER FOUR

INCLUSION

The first set of lessons address Knowledge and Understanding. Through various exercises, the students will develop a deeper understanding of the word inclusion. This increased knowledge will evolve into the significance and importance of the act of inclusion. Consolidation phase is differentiated in K-1, Gr. 2-3 activities.

KNOWLEDGE AND UNDERSTANDING -develop a deeper level of understanding of the meaning of inclusion -understand the significance of acts of inclusion	THINKING
COMMUNICATION	APPLICATION

LESSON 1

MINDS ON

Reread *Hannah's Little Sis* to the class. Generate conversation that highlights Tempest's attempts at "helping" Zack (e.g., opening the door for him, getting him paper etc.). Discuss her motives with the class. Is this an example of inclusion? Have students express and defend their opinions.

ACTION

Graffiti Wall -- In groups, have students create a one or two word or pictorial representation of inclusion. Have them put sticky notes on chart paper. Teacher reviews class opinions as to what inclusion means to them.

Through this dialogue, create a class definition of inclusion. (Oxford dictionary states inclusion is, "...the practice or policy of providing for people who might otherwise be excluded or marginalized, such as those who have physical or mental disabilities and members of minority groups." Oxford Dictionary - Oxford University Press, 2021). Post class definition in the room.

CONSOLIDATION

Discuss various scenes from the books. Have students identify if the scene involves inclusion or not. Once again, focus on evidence from the text, through dialogue.

Note: Answers are always valid if supported by evidence from the text.

Teacher Talk: Let's look at some scenes that happened in each book. Did the scene show inclusion or not? Explain your thinking.

Discuss various scenes from the books (examples on following pages). Have students identify the possible feelings associated with the scenario. Have them create a more inclusive scene with any characters from the story. Again, these are just examples of possible answers.

Teacher Talk: Let's look at some scenes that happened in each book. How do you think the character is feeling? How could you change the scene so it is more inclusive?

K-I

CONSOLIDATION (APPENDIX D1)

Scenario	Inclusion Yes and Why?	Inclusion No and Why?
HANNAH'S HUGS Hannah falls asleep with her keeper leaf in her cocoon.		
HANNAH'S LITTLE SIS Tommy asks Zack to coach the soccer team.		
KEVIN'S STRUGGLE Kevin draws the migration journey map for the class.		
RYLIE THE RIDDLER Rylie explains his ADHD at the campfire.		
BELIEVE IN BRUNO Bruno plays games with his classmates.		
READY, SET STOP! Kim and Damian help Bruno prepare for the Triple B Games.		

EXAMPLE - CONSOLIDATION

Scenario	Inclusion Yes and Why?	Inclusion No and Why?
HANNAH'S HUGS Hannah falls asleep with her keeper leaf in her cocoon.		No, she found a way to deal with her anxiety.
HANNAH'S LITTLE SIS Tommy asks Zack to coach the soccer team.	Yes, he is being included as part of the team.	
KEVIN'S STRUGGLE Kevin draws the migration journey map for the class.		No, he is just being kind to the class.
RYLIE THE RIDDLER Rylie explains his ADHD at the campfire.		No, he's just explaining something about himself to the group.
BELIEVE IN BRUNO Bruno plays games with his classmates.	Yes, he has found a way to include them in a game he wants to play.	
READY, SET STOP! Kim and Damian help Bruno prepare for the Triple B Games.	Yes, they are helping him so he can be included in the games.	No, they were being good friends.

Scenario	Make It An Inclusive Scene
HANNAH'S HUGS Hannah hides her anxiety about small spaces from her friends.	
HANNAH'S LITTLE SIS Tempest gets angry with Tommy's words about why Zack can't play soccer.	
KEVIN' STRUGGLE Kevin doesn't want anyone to know why he hides his puffer.	
RYLIE THE RIDDLER Rylie keeps forgetting things. Can his friends help him?	
BELIEVE IN BRUNO Some of the kids don't know what to do when Bruno gets upset.	
READY, SET, STOP! Kim and Damian know Bruno is a champion. How can they help others see that, too?	

EXAMPLE - CONSOLIDATION

Scenario	Make It An Inclusive Scene
HANNAH'S HUGS Hannah hides her anxiety about small spaces from her friends.	Mrs. Monarch could have a class discussion about our fears and how everyone has them. Maybe Hannah would feel more comfortable sharing her anxiety if she hears her friends have fears, too.
HANNAH'S LITTLE SIS Tempest gets angry with Tommy's words about why Zack can't play soccer. (Hannah's Little Sis)	Instead of getting angry at Tommy, Tempest could have asked him to brainstorm with her about ways to include Zack.
KEVIN' STRUGGLE Kevin doesn't want anyone to know why he hides his puffer.	
RYLIE THE RIDDLER Rylie keeps forgetting things. Can his friends help him?	
BELIEVE IN BRUNO Some of the kids don't know what to do when Bruno gets upset.	
READY, SET, STOP! Kim and Damian know Bruno is a champion. How can they help others see that, too?	

The second set of lessons address Thinking. Through various exercises, students will identify the impact acts of inclusion can have. Students explain what they would do in given situations. What impact would their behaviour have on others and self? Thus, addressing identifying and managing emotions, and expressing their feelings and understanding the feelings of others from the SEL curriculum.

KNOWLEDGE AND UNDERSTANDING	THINKING
-develop a deeper level of understanding of the meaning of inclusion -understand the significance of acts of inclusion	-students will discover different perceptions of inclusion through personal experiences -they will elicit the impact of inclusion personally and on others
COMMUNICATION	APPLICATION

LESSON 2

MINDS ON

Students will be introduced to the acts of inclusion through videos. These are examples for your use. Unpack the messages for each video, i.e., examine the feelings/emotions exhibited by the characters.

Franklin Delivers/Franklin's Shell Trouble - video about inclusion (20+ mins).
https://www.youtube.com/watch?v=fY29g4_aqAQ

Kids Talk About Inclusion - interviewers ask students of all ages what inclusion means (filmed in Australia).
https://www.youtube.com/watch?v=cYpd1_XR5pg

Kids Talk About Inclusion - interviewers ask students of all ages what inclusion means (filmed in Australia).
https://www.youtube.com/watch?v=cYpd1_XR5pg

We Are All Different - and THAT'S AWESOME! - A young ten year old boy presents a TED talk about his personal experience with inclusion.
https://www.youtube.com/watch?v=sQuM5e0QGLg

LESSON 2

ACTION

Finish the Book:

Read sections of the books provided (examples only). Read the exclusion behaviour and stop before the message turns to inclusion. Have students complete the story. Discuss the feelings/impact associated with inclusion vs. exclusion.

Teachers read up to the point before the message turns into one of inclusion. Have students finish the story with a partner via pictures and/or words.

Students showcase their scenes through a class Gallery Walk.

Teachers read up to the point before the message in the book turns into one of inclusion. Students identify the emotions/impact on the character. They write the ending through an inclusive lens in groups.

Students showcase their scenes through a class Gallery Walk.

ACTION

Resources for Finish the Book:

- *Chrysanthemum*, Kevin Henkes (Greenwillow, 1991)
- *Oliver Button Is a Sissy*, Tomie de Paola (Harcourt Brace, 1979)
- *Strictly No Elephants*, Lisa Mantchev (Simon & Schuster, 2015)

- *The Hundred Dresses*, Eleanor Estes (Harcourt Brace, 1974)
- *Thank You, Dr. Martin Luther King Jr.!* Eleanora Tate (Bantam, 1992)
- *The Name Jar*, Yangsook Choi (Dragonfly Books, 2003)

LESSON 2

CONSOLIDATION

Create a Class Book:

K-1
As a class create your own inclusive story. This is a good time to introduce or review the parts of a story (beginning, middle, end). Students can discuss ideas, characters, scenes of inclusion as a whole. Teacher records words/dialogue in the story on chart paper, then the class of "illustrators" are assigned a section of the book. Bind the finished product and donate it to the school library.

2-3
In groups of 3-4, have students create their own inclusive story. This is a good time to review the parts of a story (beginning, middle end, problem, solution). Differentiated templates are provided to help students organize their collective thoughts. Bind ("publish") the finished products and students can share with their K-1 reading buddies.

Extension: Read *Where Oliver Fits* by Cale Atkinson (Penguin Random House, 2017). Pose the question: Knowing what Oliver has learned, what advice do you think he would give to someone else trying to fit in? Can they include a similar POV in their stories?

CONSOLIDATION (APPENDICES D3, D4)

Create a Class Book:

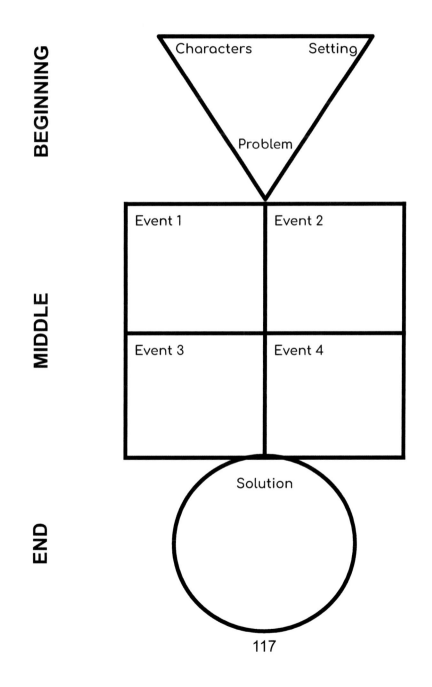

BEGINNING

Characters   Setting

Problem

MIDDLE

Event 1 | Event 2

Event 3 | Event 4

END

Solution

EXAMPLE

Characters
Amir
Simon
Charlie

Setting
At school during recess.

Problem
Charlie wants to play soccer while all his friends want to play Four Square.

Event 1
Charlie brings his new soccer ball to show his friends hoping they'll play.

Event 2
His friends go play Four square. Charlie spends this recess looking for his brother to play.

Event 3
Charlie's brother is busy with his friends and Charlie feels left out.

Event 4
Charlie practises his foot skills on the soccer field by himself.

Solution
Each recess someone different decides what the group will play.

The third set of lessons address Communication. Through various exercises, students will examine different examples of media. They will rework the piece to make their chosen picture an inclusive one.

KNOWLEDGE AND UNDERSTANDING	THINKING
-develop a deeper level of understanding of the meaning of inclusion -understand the significance of acts of inclusion	-students will discover different perceptions of inclusion through personal experiences -they will elicit the impact of inclusion personally and on others
COMMUNICATION	APPLICATION
-communicate inclusion by reworking a piece of media to address a more inclusive audience	

LESSON 3

MINDS ON

Provide examples of media ads and discuss who is left out, or not represented. Address each ad (again these are just examples, you may find some that are more pertinent to your class demographic) as a whole class conversation. Record student responses. (APPENDIX D5)

Would boys like this ad? 	Would adults like this ad? 
Would girls like this ad? 	Would children in wheelchairs like this ad? 

LESSON 3

MINDS ON

Provide examples of media ads and discuss who is left out, or not represented. Below are some examples for you to use:

Provide printed ads and access to digital ads. Have students work in groups of three and identify three ads that are exclusionary. Each group will share out about their chosen ads. They should explain the ad and who could be better represented. (APPENDIX D6)

LESSON 3

ACTION/CONSOLIDATION

Your classroom has transformed into an advertising agency. Students can decide on what they would like to name their inclusive advertising company.

As a class, brainstorm a list of products and examples of each product.

Divide students into teams. Students will work with their advertising team to create an ad for a product of their choice in differentiated platforms (posters, commercials, through STEM creations, etc.). How can their ad include as many people as possible?

Each team showcases and explains their ad to the class..

LESSON 3 - **ACTION/CONSOLIDATION**

Students choose one group to focus on for peer feedback via the butterfly template. On the left wings, identify the team and their product and item they advertised. On the right wing, draw the team members and why their ad was inclusive. (APPENDIX D7)

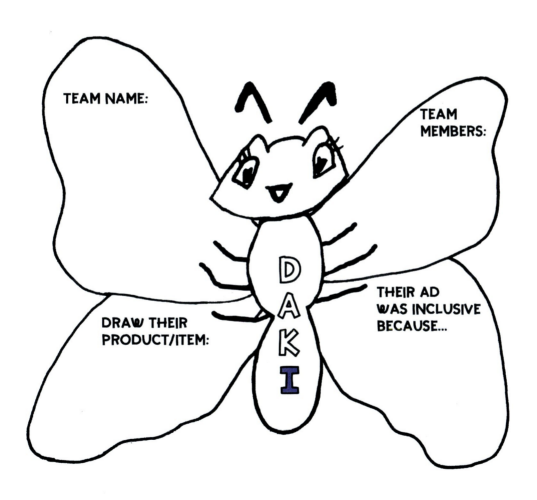

123

EXAMPLE

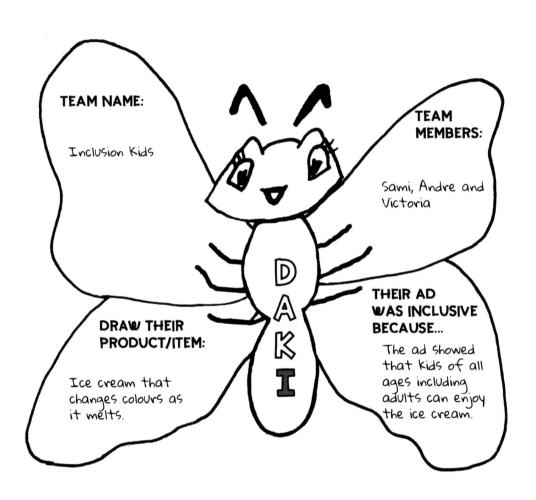

TEAM NAME:

Inclusion Kids

TEAM MEMBERS:

Sami, Andre and Victoria

DRAW THEIR PRODUCT/ITEM:

Ice cream that changes colours as it melts.

THEIR AD WAS INCLUSIVE BECAUSE...

The ad showed that kids of all ages including adults can enjoy the ice cream.

D A K I

LESSON 3

ACTION/CONSOLIDATION

Your classroom has transformed into an advertising agency. Students can decide on what they would like to name their inclusive advertising company.

As a class, brainstorm a list of products and examples of each product. Divide the class into teams. The team must come to a consensus on one product and one item.

Students will work with their advertising team to create an ad for a product of their choice in differentiated platforms (posters, commercials, through STEM creations, etc.)

Students will share and show their finished ads.

2-3 LESSON 3

ACTION/CONSOLIDATION (APPENDIX D8)

Each team signs up for a product and specific item(s) of their choice.

OUR INCLUSIVE ADVERTISING COMPANY:

NAME _____

Our Advertising Teams

Team 1 Name	Members:
Team 2 Name	Members:
Team 3 Name	Members:
Team 4 Name	Members:
Team 5 Name	Members:
Team 6 Name	Members:

PRODUCT	ITEMS

LESSON 3 - ACTION/CONSOLIDATION

Students choose two groups to focus on for peer feedback via the butterfly template. On the left wing, identify the team, members and their product and item they advertised. On the right wing, indicate why their product was inclusive. (APPENDIX D9)

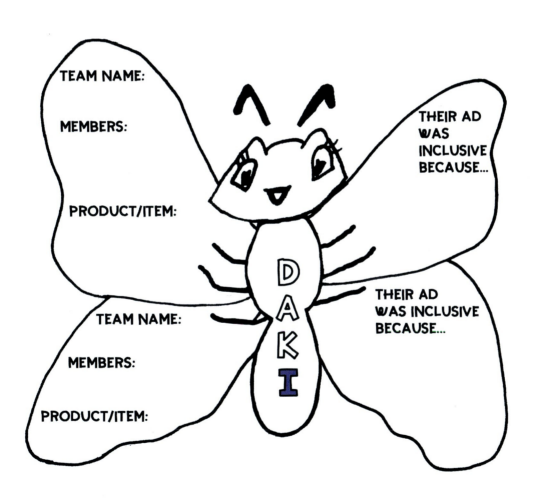

EXAMPLE

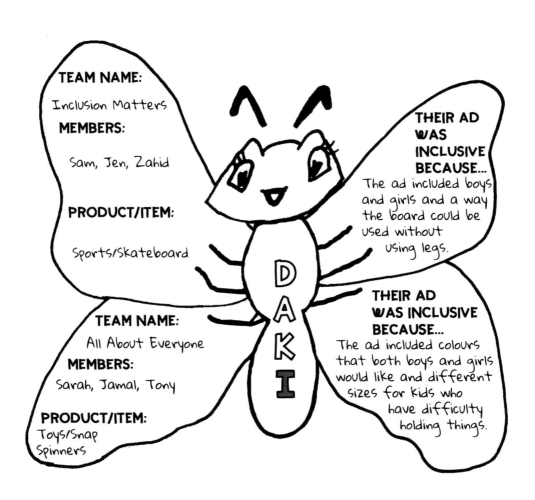

TEAM NAME:

Inclusion Matters

MEMBERS:

Sam, Jen, Zahid

PRODUCT/ITEM:

Sports/Skateboard

THEIR AD WAS INCLUSIVE BECAUSE...

The ad included boys and girls and a way the board could be used without using legs.

TEAM NAME:

All About Everyone

MEMBERS:

Sarah, Jamal, Tony

PRODUCT/ITEM:

Toys/Snap Spinners

THEIR AD WAS INCLUSIVE BECAUSE...

The ad included colours that both boys and girls would like and different sizes for kids who have difficulty holding things.

DAKI

The final lesson addresses Application. Through a culminating task, students will participate in a STEM Challenge. They will apply knowledge about inclusion and make text-to-world connections to create an inclusive playground.

KNOWLEDGE AND UNDERSTANDING	THINKING
-develop a deeper level of understanding of the meaning of inclusion -understand the significance of acts of inclusion	-students will discover different perceptions of inclusion through personal experiences -they will elicit the impact of inclusion personally and on others
COMMUNICATION	APPLICATION
-communicate inclusion by reworking a piece of media to better address inclusion	-make text-to-world connections through a STEM challenge -create an inclusive playground, accessible to all children

LESSON 4 - CULMINATING TASK

Curriculum Expectations Covered:

- Science (**Understanding Structures and Mechanisms**)
- Math (Spatial Sense: measurement, 3D solids)
- Language Arts - letter writing, persuasive writing

STEM CHALLENGE:

Using recyclable materials or building materials available, students design and build an all inclusive, accessible playground for all children to enjoy.
(See Figures 4.1 - 4.4)

Suggestions for discussions prior to the design and build:

- What equipment or play areas do you enjoy when you're at the park?
- How could those equipment items or play areas be created so that ALL children of varying abilities are included? Consider different neurodiversities, physical abilities, etc.

EXTENSION:

Have students write to their local mayor to advocate for inclusive parks in their neighbourhoods. (See Figure 4.5)

♦ Figure 4.1

♦ Figure 4.2

♦ Figure 4.3

♦ Figure 4.4

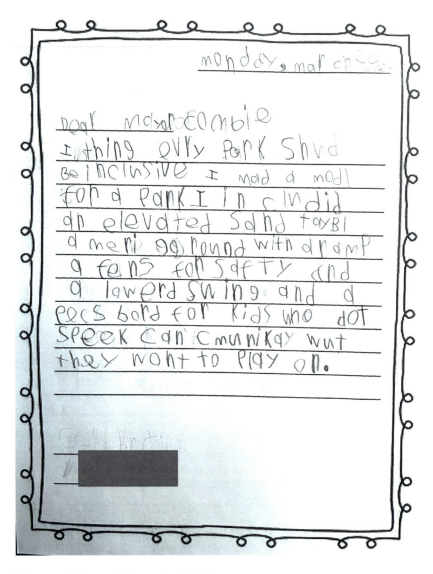

♦ **Figure 4.5** Sample letter to local Mayor.

Dear Mayor Crombie,
I think every park should be inclusive. I made a model for a park. I included an elevated sand table, a merry go round with a ramp, a fence for safety and a lowered swing and a PECS board for kids who do not speak can communicate what they want to play on.

Afterword

As a teacher for more than 20 years, I can say that I have learned more from my students, than they have learned from me. Interpreting and developing the curriculum into engaging, student-friendly lessons was a given. The part that was not so straight-forward was learning about the many different personalities and needs of my students and then creating a safe and caring space that honoured their differences, strengths and learning paths. I often wished there was a resource that I could turn to for help.

Authors Kelly Leslie and Joyce Tam have combined their collective wisdom, experiences and understanding of students in *Do the DAKI*, a social-emotional (SEL) program for K-3 educators. This year, perhaps more than any other, it is important that we build a classroom community that is respectful and inclusive of all learners, that honours the varied learning experiences of students over the past two years.

Through heart-warming picture books written by Kelly, we meet a variety of protagonists who share their strengths but also reveal what we come to learn as their positive differences. It is these differences that shape their identity, build resilience and make the world a better place.

As we head back into our classrooms, we need to remember that while we are required to teach the curriculum, we also need to take care of our students' social emotional needs. Too often we assume children inherently know how to interact with one another, but that is not always the case. Children need to be provided with opportunities to experience authentic interactions with one another in a respectful and nurturing environment. Kelly and Joyce's four pillars, pursuing positive differences, acceptance, kindness and inclusion are exactly what educators need to value individual identity, promote positive connections and build community within their classrooms. Let's embrace *Do The DAKI* and make this year the beginning of something powerful!

Sue Oolup is a primary classroom teacher with 20+ years of experience, including that of teacher-librarian. Her passions for literacy and learning about SEL have helped her to develop relationships with her students. These connections are the reasons she loves her profession.

APPENDICES

CHAPTER 1

DIFFERENCES

APPENDICES

POSITIVE DIFFERENCES #1

1. What are these? Tell me one thing about each one.

2. What positive things do you see about the sundae and the triple scoops on a waffle cone that make them the same?

3. What positive things do you see about the sundae and the triple scoops on a waffle cone that make them **different**?

4. Explain how each of their positive **differences** makes them special.

POSITIVE DIFFERENCES #2

1. What are these? Tell me one thing about each one.

2. Let's give each one a name (consensus building).

3. What positive things do you see about (insert names here) that make them the same?

4. What positive things do you see about (insert names here) that make them **different**?

5. Explain how each of their positive **differences** makes them special.

POSITIVE DIFFERENCES #3

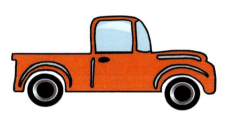 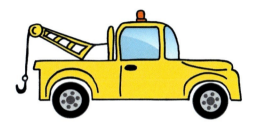

1. What are these? Tell me one thing about each one.

2. What positive things do you see about the pickup truck and the tow truck that make them the same?

3. What positive things do you see about the pickup truck and the tow truck that make them **different**?

4. Explain how each of their positive **differences** makes them special.

POSITIVE DIFFERENCES #4

1. What are these? Tell me one thing about each one.

2. What positive things do you see about the baseball and the soccer ball that make them the same?

3. What positive things do you see about the baseball and the soccer ball that make them **different**?

4. Explain how each of their positive **differences** makes them special.

POSITIVE DIFFERENCES #5

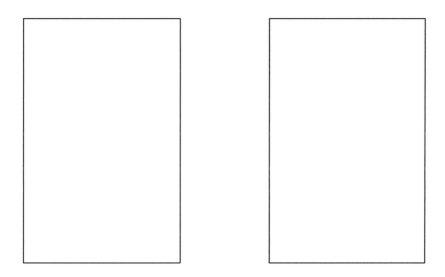

1. What are these? Tell me one thing about each one.

2. What positive things do you see about

   _____ and _____ that make them the same?

3. What positive things do you see about

   _____ and _____ that make them **different**?

4. Explain how each of their **positive differences** makes them special.

Positive Differences

Sort the pictures into the columns according to Tempest and Zack's positive differences, otherwise known as their strengths.

Positive Differences

Cards for sorting to accompany APPENDIX A6.

leader	gets things done
positive about own strengths	smart
never gives up	school
artist	soccer
funny	confident
able to see where the players belong on the field	helpful
able to see each player's strengths	uses her voice
caterpillar	caring

HANNAH'S LITTLE SIS

Positive Differences

HANNAH'S LITTLE SIS
KEVIN'S STRUGGLE

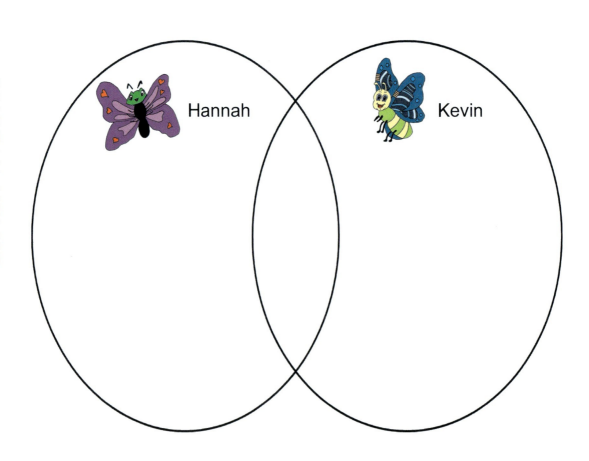

Hannah

Kevin

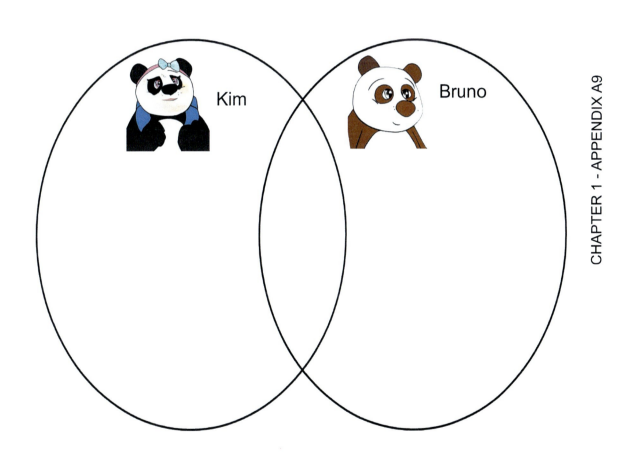

Positive Differences

BELIEVE IN BRUNO

Positive Differences

HANNAH'S LITTLE SIS
RYLIE THE RIDDLER

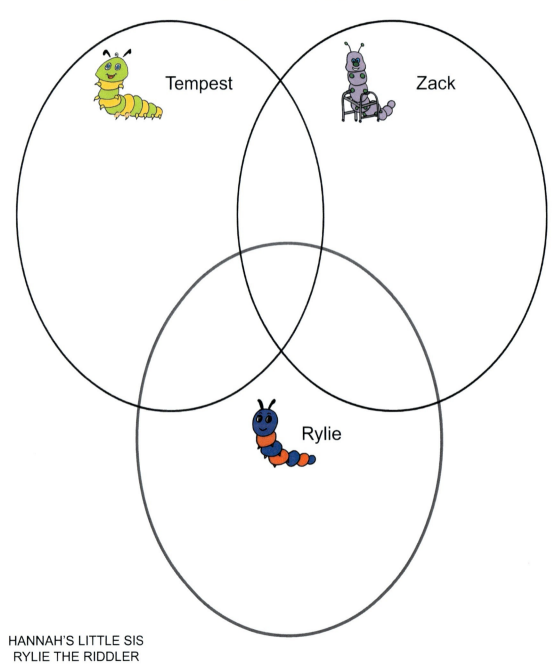

Tempest

Zack

Rylie

Positive Differences

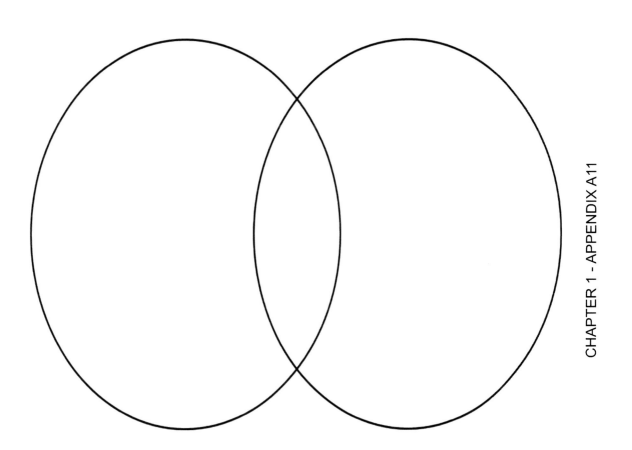

Positive Differences

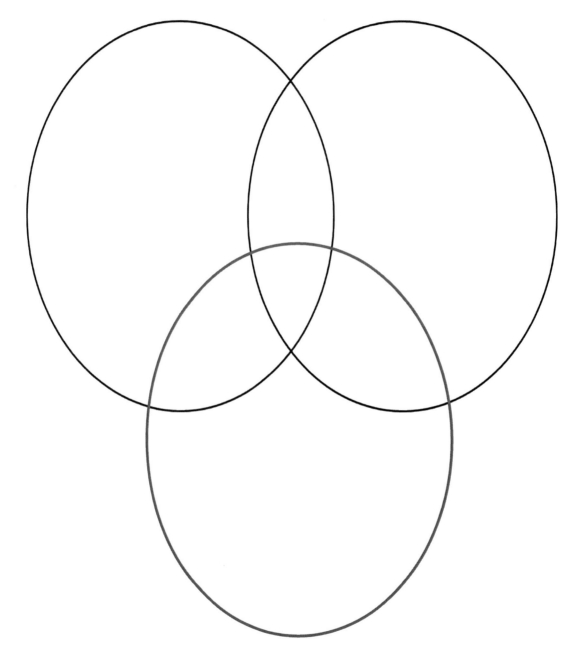

We All Have Positive Differences...
What Are Mine?

What do you like to do? What are you good at? Put one strength (**positive difference**) in each bubble.

Who Is Most Like Me?

Tempest	-caring -gets things done -never gives up -helpful -uses her voice
Zack	-able to see where the soccer players belong on the field -able to see each player's strength -good artist -funny -smart -accepts himself -positive about his strengths -confident -leader
Hannah	-caring -supportive -can relate to Kevin's struggle -helpful -uses her brain to help Kevin make the inhaler holder -is a good friend -never gives up

Who Is Most Like Me?

Kevin	-smart, especially when he makes maps -athletic (good at flying) -tries to solve his own problem -leader -thinks about things -listens
Bruno	-likes superheroes -works very hard to learn -wants friends and to be included -is a learner -kind -learning to follow directions
Kim	-kind -caring -brave -doesn't give up -accepts everyone -likes helping others
Rylie	-lots of energy -funny -super fast thinker -can solve problems really well -really good at self-talk -likes helping others

My Twin (Character) and Me

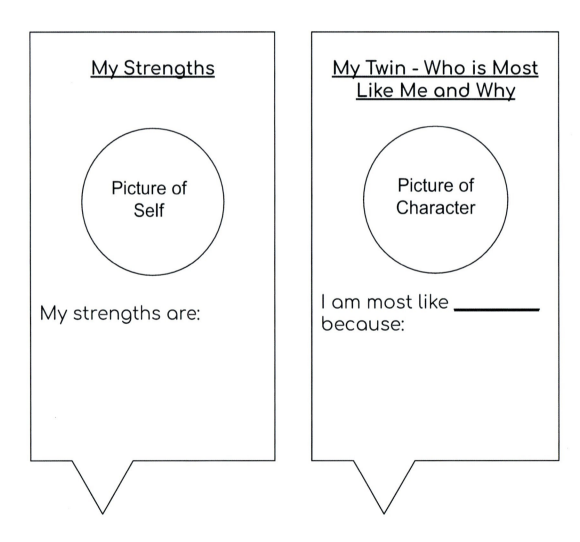

My Strengths

Picture of
Self

My strengths are:

My Twin - Who is Most
Like Me and Why

Picture of
Character

I am most like _____
because:

Draw a picture of you and your twin on the left wings.
Identify your individual strengths on the right wings.

Matching Positive Differences

Match the character to the positive difference traits. More than one trait can be connected to a character. One has been done for you.

kind
supportive
smart
athletic
fast thinker
speaks up for others
funny
energetic
caring
includes others
leader
good listener
hard worker

Matching Positive Differences

Come up with your own words and match the character to the positive difference traits. More than one trait can be connected to a character. One has been done for you.

_____

_____

_____

_____

_____

_____

_____

_____

_____

_____

_____

hard worker

Our Awesome Team

Every person on a team is what makes it awesome! Share one **positive difference** made by each person on your team. For example, Ariya, you were helpful with your organizational skills in getting everyone started. Jeremiah, your ability to spatially visualize helped the team.

As a team, match each member to one positive difference.

Positive Differences   Team Member

_____   _____

_____   _____

_____   _____

_____   _____

_____   _____

_____   _____

CHAPTER 2

ACCEPTANCE

APPENDICES

What are some things you're good at? What are some things you're still learning or working on? Include at least three things in each column.

Things I am good at...	Things I am still learning...

Choose two things you are still working on or still learning. What could you say to yourself to encourage yourself?

Things I am still learning...	Positive Self-Talk
I am still learning to	I can say
I am still learning to	I can say

Identify two things you are learning on the left wings, and what positive words you could say to yourself to keep trying, on the right wings.

What are some things your friend does that makes you like him/her so much?

Which characters from the books have some of the same behaviours as you, or your friend? Who are they and what do they do to show acceptance of others?

This is

In *Rylie The Riddler*, Rylie led the team in rescuing the primary caterpillars. Think about all the characters we know from the books. Who do you think would say the following? Draw a picture of each of them.

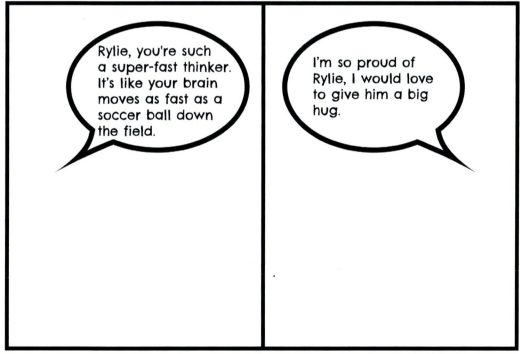

Rylie, you're such a super-fast thinker. It's like your brain moves as fast as a soccer ball down the field.

I'm so proud of Rylie, I would love to give him a big hug.

In *Rylie The Riddler*, Rylie led the team in rescuing the primary caterpillars. Think about all the characters we know from the books. Who do you think would say the following? Draw a picture of each of them.

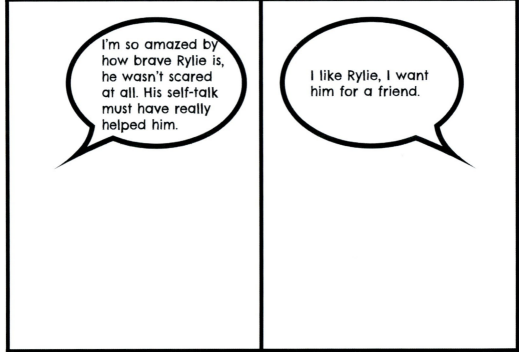

I'm so amazed by how brave Rylie is, he wasn't scared at all. His self-talk must have really helped him.

I like Rylie, I want him for a friend.

Insert your own examples from the books.

In *Rylie The Riddler*, Rylie led the team in rescuing the primary caterpillars. Think about what each character would say to Rylie from their point of view, and based on their own individual strengths. Why would their words be different?

Kevin

Zack

In *Rylie The Riddler*, Rylie led the team in rescuing the primary caterpillars. Think about what each character would say to Rylie from their point of view, and based on their own individual strengths. Why would their words be different?

CHAPTER 2 - APPENDIX B10

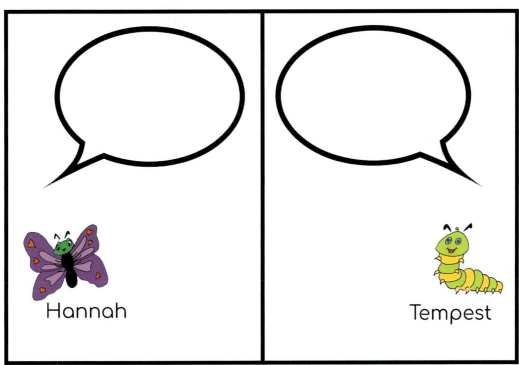

Hannah

Tempest

In *Rylie The Riddler*, Rylie led the team in rescuing the primary caterpillars. Think about what each character would say to Rylie from their point of view, and based on their own individual strengths. Why would their words be different?

Kim

Bruno

Select an opinion that you **disagree** with, the most. Find evidence from the text to prove your opposing opinion. Choose a way to show it.

EXIT TICKET

You've just completed a creative piece to support an opinion you feel strongly about. As a result, what is the POSITIVE IMPACT this could have on you and on others?

_____

_____

_____

EXIT TICKET

You've just completed a creative piece to support an opinion you feel strongly about. As a result, what is the POSITIVE IMPACT this could have on you and on others?

_____

_____

_____

CHAPTER 3

KINDNESS

APPENDICES

Identify an act of kindness you have received and one that you have have given on the left wings. What feelings or emotions did you experience as a result? Write or draw the impact on the right wings.

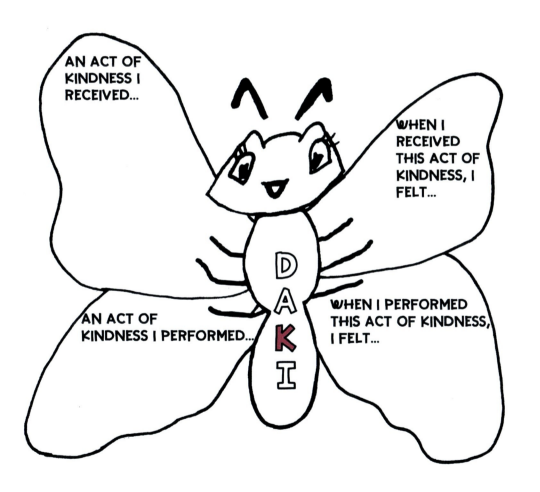

What was the act of kindness in each book?

PROBLEMS	ACTS OF KINDNESS	ANSWERS
HANNAH'S HUGS Hannah is scared to go into her cocoon.	What act of kindness did Kyle perform?	
HANNAH'S LITTLE SIS The team needs coaching.	What act of kindness did Zack perform?	
KEVIN'S STRUGGLE Kevin couldn't carry his inhaler during the long migration	What act of kindness did Hannah perform?	
RYLIE THE RIDDLER The primary caterpillars are stuck in their tent during the storm.	What act of kindness did Rylie perform?	
BELIEVE IN BRUNO Bruno becomes upset at school.	What act of kindness did Kim perform?	
READY, SET, STOP! Bruno isn't able to participate in the Triple B Games due to safety reasons.	What act of kindness do Kim and Damian perform?	

How do the characters feel before and after the act of kindness. Colour the emoji you feel best represents the feeling.

Problems	How does the character feel?	Act of Kindness	How does the character feel after?
HANNAH'S HUGS Hannah is scared to go into her cocoon.	sad / scared or worried	After Kyle hugs Hannah.	calm / happy
HANNAH'S LITTLE SIS The team needs coaching.	sad / scared or worried	After Zack becomes the soccer coach.	calm / happy
KEVIN'S STRUGGLE Kevin couldn't carry his inhaler during the long migration.	sad / scared or worried	After Hannah helps Kevin build a holder for his inhaler for the migration trip.	calm / happy

CHAPTER 3 - APPENDIX C3

K-1 How do the characters feel before and after the act of kindness. Colour the emoji you feel best represents the feeling.

Problems	How does the character feel?	Act of Kindness	How does the character feel after?
RYLIE THE RIDDLER The primary caterpillars are stuck in their tent during the storm.	sad / scared or worried	After Rylie leads the rescue of the primary caterpillars.	calm / happy
BELIEVE IN BRUNO Bruno becomes upset at school.	sad / scared or worried	After Kim befriends Bruno.	calm / happy
READY, SET, STOP! Bruno isn't able to participate in the Triple B Games due to safety concerns.	sad / scared or worried	After Kim and Damian prepare Bruno for the Triple B Games..	calm / happy

Identify the cause and effect relationship.

What is the impact as a result of the acts of kindness?

Book Title/Act of Kindness	Impact
HANNAH'S HUGS Hannah hugged her little sister when she fell and scraped her knees.	
HANNAH'S LITTLE SIS Tommy asked Zack to be a coach for the team	
KEVIN'S STRUGGLE Kevin worked really hard and created a new map for his class	
RYLIE THE RIDDLER Rylie saved the primary caterpillars	
BELIEVE IN BRUNO Kim taught her classmates ways to play with Bruno	
READY, SET, STOP! Bruno drew a picture for Kim	

Use the acts of kindness from the books to decide whether these acts are easy or hard to perform and how they impact others.

Act of Kindness	How hard is it to do? easy or hard	What is the IMPACT? (write a sentence)	Number Impacted one or many	IMPACT big or little?
HANNAH'S LITTLE SIS Tempest opens the door for Zack.				
BELIEVE IN BRUNO Kim picks up Bruno's superhero card.				
HANNAH'S LITTLE SIS Zack coaches the team.				

Act of Kindness	How hard is it to do? easy or hard	What is the IMPACT? (write a sentence)	Number Impacted one or many	IMPACT big or little?
KEVIN'S STRUGGLE Hannah encourages Kevin to share about his asthma.				
KEVIN'S STRUGGLE Kevin makes a map for the migration journey.				
RYLIE THE RIDDLER: Rylie creates a team to lift the fallen branch.				
READY, SET, STOP! Bruno draws a picture for Kim.				
Come up with your own example:				

COMPANY OF KINDNESS

Your business plan for your company's act of kindness. Remember it must impact someone, or a group, in your community.

VP Names	
Company Name	
Plan/Idea - Act of Kindness	
Who Will It Impact, and How?	
Company Logo (Design)	

Parts to create a Kindness Caterpillar.

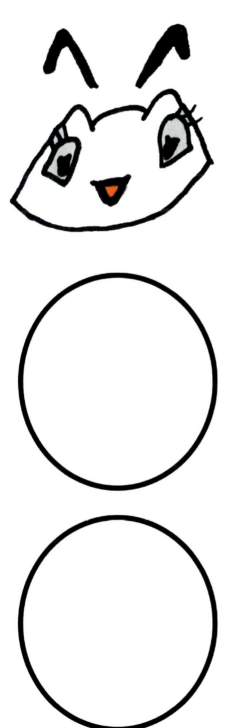

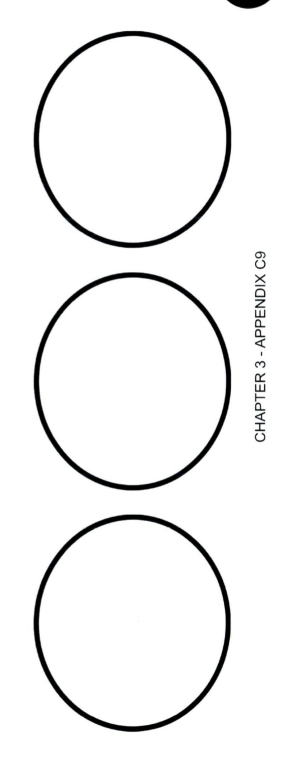

The VPs of each company will pitch their idea to the Board of Directors (i.e., present their business plan to the class). Below is an example of a rubric for this assessment.

COMPANY OF KINDNESS RUBRIC

Categories	Level 4	Level 3	Level 2	Level 1
Knowledge and Understanding	Demonstrated a clear and cohesive understanding of their chosen act of kindness and the scale of its impact on a community	Demonstrated understanding of their chosen act of kindness and its impact on a community	Demonstrated understanding of their chosen act of kindness and its impact on a community, with support	Began to demonstrate understanding of their chosen act of kindness and its impact on a community, with support
Thinking	Planned a detailed Company of Kindness action plan and was cognizant of the critical thinking skills used (i.e., making inferences)	Planned and applied critical thinking skills to develop a Company of Kindness action plan	Planned and applied critical thinking skills to develop a Company of Kindness action plan, with support	Began to plan a Company of Kindness action plan, with support
Communication	Organized and expressed ideas in business plan and advertisement, with creativity and detail	Organized and expressed ideas in business plan and advertisement	Organized and expressed ideas in business plan and advertisement, with support	Began to organize and express ideas in business plan and advertisement, with support
Application	Made meaningful connections between Company of Kindness action plan and the impact it would have on their chosen community	Made connections between Company of Kindness action plan and the impact it would have on their chosen community	Made connections between Company of Kindness action plan and the impact it would have on their chosen community, with support	Began to make connections between Company of Kindness action plan and the impact it would have on their chosen community, with support

OUR ACT OF KINDNESS
PLANNING SHEET

Team Name:

Act of Kindness:	
Materials:	
Jobs:	
Group One (Names)	
Group Two (Names)	
Group Three (Names)	
Group Four (Names)	
Group Four (Names)	

CHAPTER 4

INCLUSION

APPENDICES

Do the scenes show that everyone was included?
Explain our thinking.

Scenario	Inclusion Yes and Why?	Inclusion No and Why?
HANNAH'S HUGS Hannah falls asleep with her keeper leaf in her cocoon.		
HANNAH'S LITTLE SIS Tommy asks Zack to coach the soccer team.		
KEVIN'S STRUGGLE Kevin draws the migration journey map for the class.		
RYLIE THE RIDDLER Rylie explains his ADHD at the campfire.		
BELIEVE IN BRUNO Bruno plays games with his classmates.		
READY, SET STOP! Kim and Damian help Bruno prepare for the Triple B Games.		

2-3 Let's look at some scenes that happened in each book. How do you think the character is feeling? How could you change the scene so it is more inclusive?

Scenario	Make It An Inclusive Scene
HANNAH'S HUGS Hannah hides her anxiety about small spaces from her friends.	
HANNAH'S LITTLE SIS Tempest gets angry with Tommy's words about why Zack can't play soccer.	
KEVIN' STRUGGLE Kevin doesn't want anyone to know why he hides his puffer.	
RYLIE THE RIDDLER Rylie keeps forgetting things. Can his friends help him?	
BELIEVE IN BRUNO Some of the kids don't know what to do when Bruno gets upset.	
READY, SET, STOP! Kim and Damian know Bruno is a champion. How can they help others see that, too?	

Title:

BEGINNING

Characters   Setting

Problem

MIDDLE

Event 1	Event 2
Event 3	Event 4

END

Solution

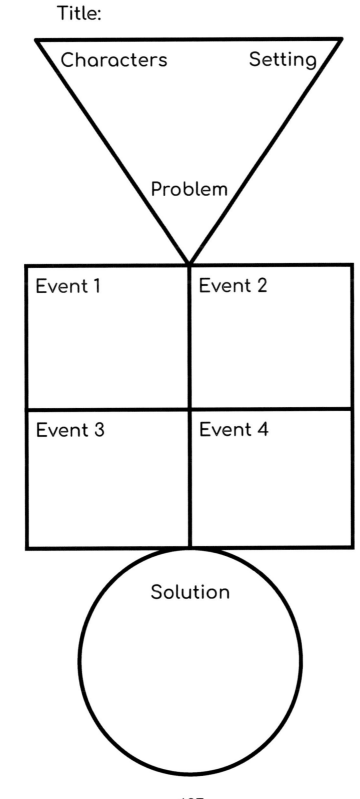

2-3

BEGINNING

Characters (WHO)	Settling (WHERE)

MIDDLE

Problem (WHAT)

END

Solution (HOW)

Provide examples of media ads and discuss who is left out. Address each ad (again these are just examples, you may find some that are more pertinent to your class demographic) as a whole class conversation. Record student responses.

Would boys like this ad?	Would adults like this ad?

Would girls like this ad?	Would children in wheelchairs like this ad?

Provide examples of media ads and discuss who is left out, or not represented.

Below are some examples for you to use:

Provide printed ads and access to digital ads. Have students work in groups of three and identify three ads that are exclusionary. Each group will share out about their chosen ads. They should explain the ad and who could be better represented.

Choose one group to focus on for peer feedback. On the left wings, identify the team and their product and item they advertised. On the right wing, draw the team members and why their ad was inclusive.

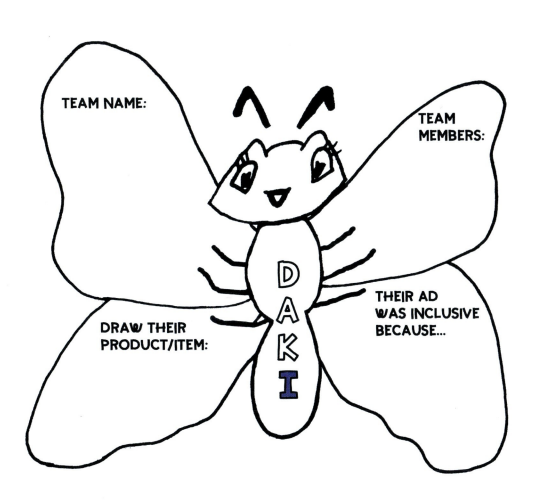

2-3

Each team signs up for a product and specific item(s) of their choice.

OUR INCLUSIVE ADVERTISING COMPANY:

NAME _____

Our Advertising Teams

Team 1 Name	Members:
Team 2 Name	Members:
Team 3 Name	Members:
Team 4 Name	Members:
Team 5 Name	Members:
Team 6 Name	Members:

PRODUCT	ITEMS

Choose two groups to focus on for peer feedback. On the left wing, identify the team, members and their product and item they advertised. On the right wing, indicate why their product was inclusive.

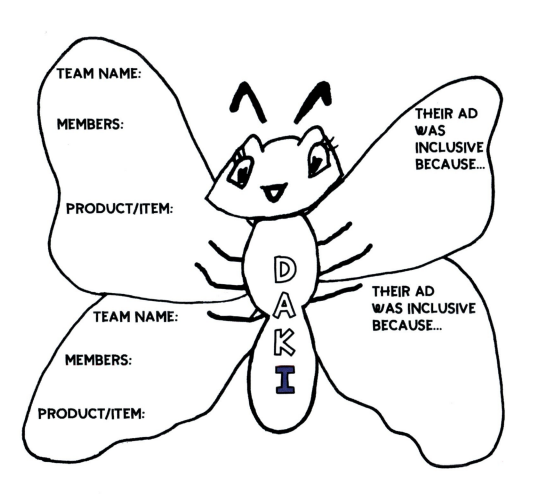

TEAM NAME:

MEMBERS:

PRODUCT/ITEM:

THEIR AD WAS INCLUSIVE BECAUSE...

TEAM NAME:

MEMBERS:

PRODUCT/ITEM:

THEIR AD WAS INCLUSIVE BECAUSE...

Resources

The next page contains templates that align with our year-long initiative. Similar to the idea, "You Got Caught Doing Something Good", the butterflies can apply to the DAKI acronym. If a teacher or student witnesses someone recognizing positive differences, showing acceptance, kindness, or inclusion, they are granted a butterfly. The black and white version are for students to decorate themselves with the pertinent letter highlighted. Teachers may wish to create a wall of butterflies showcasing the recognition of positive differences, acts of kindness, acceptance, and inclusion throughout the year.

The following page is a certificate students may be given once they have completed the DAKI program.

Available to you are activities at the back of each picture book for students to extend their thinking and understanding of the concepts presented. In addition to these picture books, there are curriculum related resources readily available to parents and educators on the KLESLIEBOOKS website to either print or assign directly to an online learning platform. Educators can find K-3 lessons connected to math, science, social studies, coding, SEL, and STEM.

sites.google.com/view/klesliebooks

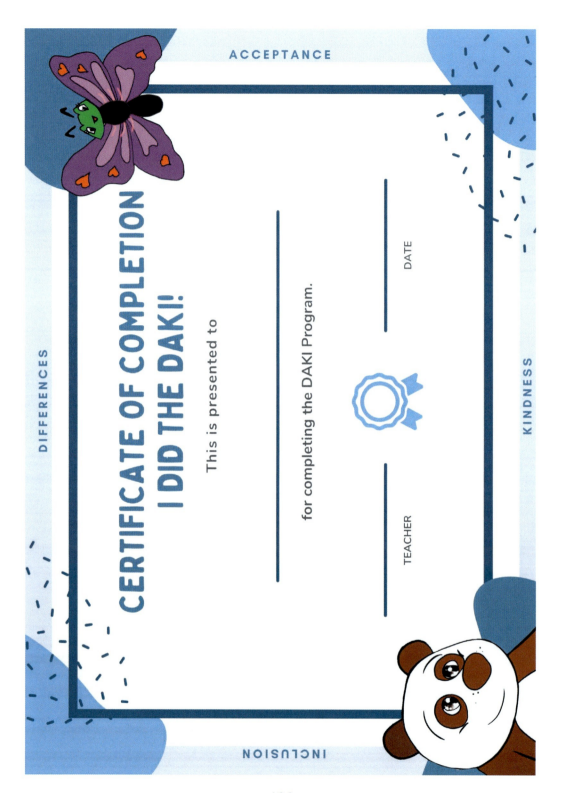

ACCEPTANCE

DIFFERENCES

CERTIFICATE OF COMPLETION
I DID THE DAKI!

This is presented to

for completing the DAKI Program.

TEACHER

DATE

KINDNESS

INCLUSION

Bibliography

Children's Books Cited:

Atkinson, C. (2017). *Where Oliver Fits.* Penguin Random House.

Choi, Y. (2003). *The Name Jar.* Dragonfly Books.

de Paola, T. (1979). *Oliver Button Is A Sissy.* Simon & Schuster.

DiOrio, R. (2009). *What Does It Mean To Be Global?* (C. Hill, Illus.). Sourcebooks.

Estes, E. (1974). *The Hundred Dresses.* (L. Slobodkin, Illus.). Harcourt Brace.

Henkes, K. (1991). *Chrysanthemum.* Harper Collins

Laundry, M. (2014). *I Can Make A Difference.* (J. Julich, Illus.). Simon & Schuster.

Leslie, K. (2020). *Hannah's Hugs.* KD Publishing.

Leslie, K. (2020). *Hannah Series: Hannah's Little Sis.* KD Publishing.

Leslie, K. (2020). *Believe in Bruno.* (M. Salisbury, Illus.). KD Publishing.

Leslie, K. (2020). *Hannah Series: Kevin's Struggle.* KD Publishing.

Leslie, K. (2021). *Hannah Series: Rylie the Riddler.* KD Publishing.

Leslie, K. (2021). *Bruno Series: Ready, Set, Stop!* (A. George, Illus.). KD Publishing.

Mantchev, L. (2015). *Strictly No Elephants.* (T. Yoo, Illus.). Simon & Schuster.

Smith-Milway, K. *One Hen.* (E. Fernandes). Bloomsbury Publishing.

Tate, E. (1992). *Thank You, Dr. Martin Luther King, Jr.* Bantam.

Thomas, P. (2002). *Don't Call Me Special.* (K. Harker, Illus.). Hauppauge, New York.

Professional Resources:

Ministry of Education. The Ontario Curriculum: *Grade 2* [Program of Studies].
    http://www.edu.gov.on.ca/eng/curriculum/elementary/ grade2.html

Ministry of Education. (2010). Growing Success: *Assessment, Evaluation, and Reporting in Ontario Schools*
http://www.edu.gov.on.ca/eng/policyfunding/growSuccess.pdf

Simpson, J., Weinar, E. (2021). *Inclusion.* Oxford Dictionary. Oxford University Press.

Videos:

"10 Random Acts of Kindness for Kids." YouTube, uploaded by The Cohen
        Show, Nov. 22, 2017,
            https://www.youtube.com/watch?v=OBbyjZdOsGo&t=27s
"Franklin Delivers/Franklin's Shell Trouble." YouTube, uploaded by Tommy
        Martin, 2019,
            https://www.youtube.com/watch?v=fY29g4_aqAQ&t=117s
"How To Make Plasticine Portraits Inspired by: Author Illustrator, Barbara
        Reid." YouTube, uploaded by Books and Brushes for Kids, Oct. 10,
        2019,
            https://www.youtube.com/watch?v=z-Kw8fhfDNQ
"Kids Talk About Inclusion." YouTube, uploaded by Diversity Kids, June 21,
        2019, https://www.youtube.com/watch?v=cYpd1_XR5pg
"We Are All Different - and THAT'S AWESOME!" YouTube, uploaded by
        TEDxWestVancouverED, Oct. 30, 2017,
            https://www.youtube.com/watch?v=sQuM5e0QGLg

Websites:

Care Canada. "Walk In Her Shoes."
            https://care.ca/fundraise-for-care/walk-in-her-shoes/
Mediavine Family. "23 Awesome Team Building Activities for Kids." The
        Queen Momma, Nov. 26, 2020,
            https://thequeenmomma.com/team-building-activities-for-kids/
United Nations. "Student Resources - United Nations Sustainable
        Development." Sustainable Development Goals, June 24, 2021
            https://www.un.org/sustainabledevelopment/student- resources/

Manufactured by Amazon.ca
Bolton, ON

20858972R00128